Contents

Introduction

The First Certificate in English

The First Certificate in English (FCE) is an examination offered by the University of Cambridge Local Examinations Syndicate. It is the most widely taken of their exams. Since it was first offered in 1939 as the Lower Certificate of Proficiency, it has been revised three times – in 1974, in 1984 and, most recently, in 1996. Significant changes were made in 1996. They involved the introduction of new question types and procedures while keeping the level and overall rationale the same. This set of Practice Tests contains material which mirrors the actual exams offered from 1996 and provides valuable information and practice for the five papers of the FCE.

For further information about UCLES exams, write to UCLES, 1 Hills Road, Cambridge, CB1 2EU, England.

Level

Students who pass FCE are expected to be able to function independently in the language in a range of situations. They are able to use and understand the main structures of English and a wide range of vocabulary, and are able to communicate in a range of social situations. A student who passes FCE should be ready to begin using English in a work environment or as a means of study.

On average, a student will be ready to take FCE after approximately 550 hours of active study of English. This obviously varies from person to person depending on their circumstances, ability, motivation, etc, but it is a rough guide.

FCE fits between the Preliminary English Test (PET) and the Certificate in Advanced English (CAE) in the suite of exams which are offered by the University of Cambridge Local Examinations Syndicate. Students who have passed PET could expect to need approximately another 200 hours of active study before they might pass FCE. (In level, PET is about two-thirds of the way to FCE.)

In addition to the required level in English, a student taking FCE needs to have the capacity to survive in the exam room as there are five papers, at least three of which are taken in one day. This requires concentration and staying power.

Structure of the examination

Paper 1	Reading	1 hour 15 mins	four texts – 35 questions
Paper 2	Writing	1 hour 30 mins	Part 1 one compulsory task, Part 2 one chosen from four tasks offered (three general and one on set books) – two writing tasks in total
Paper 3	Use of English	1 hour 15 mins	five tasks – 65 questions
Paper 4	Listening	40 mins (approx.)	two longer recorded texts and two series of short extracts – 30 questions
Paper 5	Speaking	15 mins (approx.)	An interaction between two candidates and an interlocutor/assessor. For assessment purposes a second assessor is present who takes no part in the interaction.

Special needs

Students who need special help or consideration, for example, the blind, deaf or otherwise physically disadvantaged, should contact UCLES at the address given, for information about the ways in which they can be helped to take the examination. UCLES will provide suitably modified papers and arrangements can be made for help at the time of the examination. Students with learning difficulties, for example dyslexia, may also receive special consideration if they can provide suitable documentation. Teachers should also be aware that it might be worth informing UCLES if students have had serious personal problems (such as bereavement) around the time of the exam.

Topics

The texts, speaking and writing exercises which form the basis of the First Certificate in English are drawn from a list of 25 broad topic areas. In preparing for the examination, it is advisable for students to aim to widen their vocabulary in as many of these areas as possible.

All 25 topics are represented in the eight tests which make up the present book and *Cambridge Practice Tests for First Certificate 2*. The list of specified topics is as follows:

- Personal life and circumstances e.g. personal experiences
- Living conditions e.g. where/how people live
- Occupations
- Education, study and learning
- Free-time activities
- Travel and tourism
- Consumer goods and shopping
- Eating and drinking
- Social/family relations
- The media
- The weather
- The environment/ecology
- Entertainment
- Health and exercise
- Services e.g. banks, post offices, etc.
- Places
- Language
- Music
- Fashion
- Animals
- Cinema
- History
- The Arts
- Sports
- People

A guide to the papers

Paper 1 Reading

Format

The Reading paper consists of four parts, each part containing one text (or a group of texts) along with a set of questions. **Part 1** is a multiple matching exercise (matching parts of the text to either relevant headings or summary sentences) with six or seven questions, **Part 2** is a multiple choice exercise with seven or eight questions, **Part 3** is a gapped-text exercise with six or seven questions (the gaps are either sentences or paragraphs) and **Part 4** is a multiple matching exercise (scanning a text to find specific information). The total number of questions on the paper is 35.

The tasks

The Reading paper aims to test a range of reading skills such as finding specific information and understanding gist, detail, the main idea, inference, cohesion, text structure, functional and sociolinguistic meaning. Students are encouraged to develop different reading skills in order to approach the different tasks in each part. Each task requires the employment of a range of skills but the main skill needed varies from one task to another, for example, **Part 1** requires reading for gist and detail, **Part 2** requires reading for detail and also for cohesion and global meaning, **Part 3** tests an understanding of text structure as well as reading for gist and detail and **Part 4** requires students to search for specific information. The position of the questions varies according to the nature of the task – for **Parts 1** and **4** the questions come first and for **Parts 2** and **4** the questions follow the text.

The texts

The texts come from a range of sources such as newspapers, magazines, books, brochures, leaflets and letters. These include articles, advertisements, reports, reviews, informational material, fiction and correspondence. One of the parts may contain a multi-text which consists of two or more shorter related texts. The aim is to present students with a range of real texts which they might come across in the English-speaking world. The texts are altered as little as possible but it is usually necessary to simplify some of the lexis as there are very few pieces in the real world which are written at FCE level. Texts may also be shortened. Illustrations may be used either as an aid to understanding an important concept or simply to retain the authenticity of the text. Where possible, the exam text will reflect the original in terms of layout and typeface.

The length of the texts in each part varies but is in the range of 350–700 words per text with an overall total of 1900–2300 words over the whole paper.

At first glance, the number of words may seem daunting to a student, but not all the tasks require detailed reading. When preparing students for the Reading paper it is important to explain that it is not necessary for them to understand every single word of all the texts to answer the questions. Some of the lexis, which is neither central to the task nor necessary for an understanding of the whole text, is indeed above FCE level and can either be guessed or ignored.

Preparing students

If possible, students should be shown the different text types that appear in the exam, for example, newspapers, magazines, advertisements. If English Language publications are not available, students can be encouraged to look at local newspapers and magazines in their own language and talk about the different kinds of texts. Students can look at layouts and headlines and they should realise that they can get an idea of the nature of a text before they actually start to read. It is important that they become used to reading the instructions carefully as these explain not only what they have to do but also where the text came from, for example, a magazine article.

It is a good idea to explain to students that it is best to approach each part of the paper in a different way. If they read through every word of every text before looking at the questions, they are almost certain to run out of time. In **Parts 1** and **4** they should look at the questions first.

PART 1

The questions are either headings or summary sentences which should be matched to the relevant parts of the text. There is an example, which cannot be used again. The headings or summary sentences are jumbled. When students have read through the headings or sentences, they should then start reading the text. For each part of the text, they match the corresponding heading or sentence. If they are unsure of any, they should leave them until the end when there will be fewer to choose from. There is one extra heading or sentence which does not need to be used. When all the headings or sentences have been matched, students should go back and check as it is easy to miss something the first time. They should remember that there is only one heading or sentence that does not fit anywhere. Students can practise this type of task with real newspaper articles. Newspapers usually have short paragraphs summarising the day's news and each has a heading. They will probably be quite easy to match but it will give them valuable practice in skimming for gist and matching. Students could also try writing their own headings or summary sentences for articles or passages from a course book, then jumbling them up and giving them to other students to solve.

PART 2

Students can read the text first to get an overall understanding and then go back and look at it again in more detail while answering the multiple choice questions. There will probably be at least one question testing cohesion (e.g. 'What does *it* refer to in line 6?'). For this question, students need to practise looking around the word in the text and underlining the different choices. They should then read through that part of the text again, looking for clues which connect one of the options to 'it'. There will probably be a question which tests global understanding and students should be able to answer this once they have worked through the whole text.

PART 3

One sentence has been taken out of each paragraph, or every alternate paragraph has been removed. Students may find it easiest to read what is left of the original text to get an idea of what it is about and then look at the sentences or paragraphs which have been removed. There is one extra sentence or paragraph, which is not needed. The first gap is already completed as an example. Students should be encouraged to work through the text by reading the first paragraph and then finding which sentence or paragraph fits next. They can look for words which may help them such as pronouns, time indicators, sequencing of events, geographical locations. If they are unsure what fits in a gap, they should leave that one and continue. They can come back at the end and fill in the missing ones. If they fit the wrong paragraph or sentence into a gap near the beginning, it will then make the rest of the exercise very difficult. If there is time at the end, they could check around each gap to check it makes sense with what goes before and after. There will probably not be time to read through the whole text again.

As practice, the paragraphs of other texts could be cut up or sentences deleted. At first, the task could be attempted on texts which are already familiar to students. Help them to recognise the kind of words and phrases which link paragraphs and to look out for tense changes.

PART 4

The questions come before the text and are not in the same order as the information in the text. They ask students to look for specific information. Students should be encouraged to scan the text until they find the part which is relevant. They should then slow down and read in more detail. Each part of the text can be used more than once so the same number of choices stays in play throughout the task. Students need to learn to read these texts fairly quickly and not worry about individual words which they do not understand. The skill of retrieving specific information is one we use every day when looking for a telephone number, finding out what is on television, deciding which film to go and watch from a list of reviews, etc. Students need to realise that they carry out this kind of task every day in their own language and, if possible, they should practise some real-life task in English in class. It doesn't matter if the language is too difficult for them as long as the task is within their reach – it will train them to scan text for the relevant information.

Paper 2 Writing

Format

The Writing paper lasts one hour thirty minutes and is divided into two parts. **Part 1** consists of a compulsory letter. In **Part 2**, students choose one of five tasks. The word limit is 120–180 words for each part. Students write their answers in the question paper booklet.

The tasks

In **Part 1**, students are presented with a task by means of up to three short pieces of text such as advertisements, letters, notes, leaflets, diaries, timetables or notices. They are required to write a transactional letter, i.e. one that aims to achieve a given purpose. The purpose will vary according to context, for example, they may need to impart or request information, to describe or narrate, to complain or explain, and so on. The style will be neutral or slightly formal. The addressee and the purpose of the task will always be clearly stated in the rubric. In **Part 2**, students are offered five options which will always include: at least one situationally-based task such as a letter, report or application; at least one composition of a discursive, descriptive or narrative type; two alternative tasks on the prescribed background texts (see note on *set books* below). Students are expected to produce content and style appropriate to the given reader and purpose. **Part 1** also requires students to assimilate and select from the stimulus material. This part of the paper is designed to assist in the standardisation of marking as the task is common to all students. In any single test, the tasks in **Part 2** are designed to avoid duplication of the one in **Part 1**, so students must expect to write two quite different pieces.

Preparing students

The writing skills required for the two parts of this paper are broadly the same: the ability to write generally correct (but not flawless) straightforward English which demonstrates awareness of purpose and of the target reader in terms of both content and style.

In **Part 1**, it is particularly important for students to make intelligent use of the stimulus material. They should be trained to select and re-phrase appropriately and to avoid indiscriminate lifting. As well as practising a variety of writing tasks of the correct length and under examination conditions, it is also worth students' while to measure the extent of their handwriting when preparing for the examination, so that they can judge the length of their answers without wasting valuable time counting words during the examination itself.

For both **Parts 1** and **2**, it is a good idea to train students to analyse each task by means of the questions: *What* am I writing? (letter, report, story, etc.) *Who* am I writing for? (my teacher, a possible employer, other students, etc.) *Why* am I writing? (to inform, to entertain, to complain, etc.) and to understand the implications of their answers to these questions in terms of content and style. Use of underlining or a highlighter pen is recommended at this stage. They should then ask themselves: What shall I say? and be encouraged to make a brief plan of the content of their answer before beginning to write. This will allow them to concentrate on the quality of their language as they write, rather than being distracted by the search for ideas. In **Part 2**, it will also enable them to discover, before they have wasted too much time, if they have chosen a subject which they cannot handle confidently.

Set books

Students may choose to study one or more from a list of set books and answer a question on them in **Paper 2 Part 2**. Apart from any broader interest that students and teachers may have in studying these books, the main advantage as far as the examination is concerned lies in the fact that it enables students to write about subject matter with which they are thoroughly familiar. The books are either very straightforward original texts or simplified readers of an appropriate level. Literary criticism is not expected of candidates, but the tasks are likely to involve a range of language skills. For example, they may be asked to narrate a part of the story, describe a location or person, comment on actions or motives, or give their opinion about events or behaviour. The list of set books is published by UCLES in the examination regulations and the set books are changed every two years.

Paper 3 Use of English

Format

The Use of English paper consists of five parts. **Parts 1, 2, 4** and **5** each consist of a set of questions based on a short text. **Part 3** consists of ten separate questions. **Part 1** (15 questions) is a multiple-choice cloze exercise in which students choose the correct word(s) from four options to fill gaps in a text of around 200 words. **Part 2** (15 questions) is an 'open' cloze exercise which requires students to supply their own words (one word per gap) to complete a text of around 200 words. In **Part 3** (10 questions), students must complete a gap in a sentence (between two and five words per gap) so that it means the same as the sentence printed above it. They are given one 'key' word which must form part of the answer, and which must not be altered in any way. **Part 4** (15 questions) is an error-identification exercise. Students must identify correct and incorrect lines in a text of around 200 words. For incorrect lines, the extra *and unnecessary* word causing the error must also be identified. **Part 5** (10 questions) is a word-formation exercise. Students are required to fill gaps in a text of around 150 words by creating suitable parts of speech from the root words given. This may involve, for example, forming a noun from a verb (e.g. *appear* → *appearance*), an adverb from an adjective (e.g. *fortunate* → *unfortunately*), etc.

One hour fifteen minutes is allowed for the paper, which has a total of 65 questions. Answers are recorded on a separate answer sheet.

The tasks

The paper aims to test the student's knowledge of the lexical and grammatical systems of the language by means of questions which variously require the student to identify, select or supply appropriate responses. Each of the four text-based tasks requires the student to form a general idea of the context in order to appreciate fully the requirements of the individual questions. In **Part 3**, each of the discrete-sentence pairs can be viewed as a 'mini-text' performing a similar function.

Part 1 consists mainly of lexical questions focusing on the selection of the only option with the correct meaning for the context. A small proportion of the questions will also have a grammatical element, in that two or more options may have an appropriate meaning, and the final choice will rest on the grammatical compatibility of the options with the gap in question.

The 'open' gaps in **Part 2** are designed to focus mainly on structural elements of the language. Some items will have a clear lexical element (e.g. when the correct tense of a suitable verb must be supplied), but all words required will be well within the competence of the average FCE candidate.

Part 3 combines lexical and structural elements and samples the student's ability to produce longer sequences of language to complete the expression of a given meaning in a given way. By limiting the number of successful variations for any particular gap, the key word and the word limit enable a wide range of structural points to be tested reliably.

Part 4 tests the student's ability to identify a variety of errors in a piece of connected prose. The form of the error is always that of an *extra and unnecessary word*, but a wide variety of common errors can be tested in this way.

Part 5 tests the student's ability to identify the part of speech required to fill a gap in a text and to form the correct response from a given root word. The exact form of word required may be influenced by the wider context of the piece. This may mean, for example, that a negative adjective is required, rather than a positive one.

The texts

The texts for **Paper 3** are primarily a vehicle for the testing points they contain. They offer a certain amount of intrinsic interest, but operate at a lexical and conceptual level somewhat below the texts on the Reading paper, and are not intended to pose genuine comprehension problems for competent FCE candidates.

The texts for **Parts 1, 2** and **5** generally come from original sources such as newspapers, books and magazines. They are drawn from a range of text-types including factual, narrative, descriptive, discursive, imaginative, etc., and may be based on reports, articles, fiction, correspondence, informational material and so on. Because of the strict technical and lexical requirements of the examination, it is rarely possible to use original texts without a certain amount of editing and adaptation.

The text for **Part 4** is different, in that it is intended to represent a standard of English within the competence of the best FCE students. The texts are specially composed to reflect a broad spectrum of student error, since using a single authentic source would inevitably bias the test against students who shared the original writer's first language.

Preparing students

The total reading load of the paper is in the region of 1100 words. Slower readers can be put at a disadvantage, and so, as with the Reading paper, reading speed in English is worthy of attention in preparing for the examination. Practice in reading quickly for gist is particularly helpful.

With all text-based questions, it is advisable to read quickly through the text first to form an overall impression of the context before attempting to mark any answers. Students should not neglect the 'example' sentences at the beginning, which may contain important contextual clues.

Great care should be taken with spelling throughout the paper.

Parts 1, 2, 3 and 5 are all gap-filling exercises and have certain technical points in common, which can usefully be pointed out to students.

- The majority of structural and contextual clues to the correct answer will be found in the areas immediately before **or after** the gap. All students look before the gap. Incorrect answers, however, often demonstrate the failure to recognise the need for structural or lexical cohesion with what **follows** the gap.
- 'Problem' gaps in texts may be better passed over until most of the more straightforward answers have been made. As the text nears completion, it may be easier to deal with the more difficult items.
- Students should try to leave time to read quickly through the completed text to ensure that the whole piece makes sense.

Part 1 Correct answers must have the correct meaning for the context and must fit successfully into the structure of the sentence. They may also have to form part of a collocation or other fixed phrase.

In addition to general vocabulary work, it is advantageous for FCE students to pay attention to collocations and other semantic sets as they occur in their reading and classwork.

Part 2 All the missing words are essential to the structure of the sentence from which they have been removed. Gaps can generally only be filled by one part of speech. Some gaps may have alternative answers, but these will usually be near-synonyms (e.g. *each/every; because/as/since*). Students should try to avoid wasting time choosing the best of two or three equally correct responses.

Early practice can usefully concentrate on identifying the missing part of speech. Students can gain confidence with the mechanics of the exercise by producing their own short cloze tests.

Part 3 The correct answer should preserve all important elements of the meaning from the original sentence. Students should not make unnecessary changes in vocabulary. Otherwise correct answers which alter the key word in any way or use too many words will be penalised.

Students should develop an awareness of points commonly tested, so that they have an idea of what to look out for. Grammar work should take account of the need at this level to be able to express the same idea in different ways, and to move freely from one form to another.

Part 4 Of the fifteen lines tested, between three and five will be correct. The extra words which must be identified are always clearly inappropriate, not just optional additions, and may appear anywhere in the line: this means that a word early in the line may be shown to be wrong because of something in the previous line; a word near the end may be wrong because of the continuation on the next line. For this reason, it is important to remind students that they are dealing with **a complete text**, and not fifteen separate questions.

Students should be encouraged to check their own and/or colleagues' work whenever possible. Although the form of the errors they find will not always be the same as the FCE exercise (i.e. an extra word) many of the same structural points will be tested in the examination. The improvement of self-checking is obviously of great benefit to the Writing paper as well.

Part 5 No correct answer will involve making more than two changes to the original word given (e.g. *interest* → *uninterested* can be included, *interest* → *uninterestedly* cannot). Students should remain aware of the wider context for their answers: whether a person in a text is *fortunate* or *unfortunate* may depend on elements of the text which are some distance from the gap in question.

Students should be encouraged to develop an interest in word groups, and should receive guidance on extending their use of the dictionary and modifying their own strategy for recording new vocabulary if necessary. Common word groups can be usefully and enjoyably revised in a quiz format.

Paper 4 Listening

Format

The Listening paper is presented on audio cassette. Students can write on their question papers as they listen. The Paper lasts up to 45 minutes. This includes five minutes at the end when students copy their answers onto the answer sheet (see note on p. 25). There are four parts to each test and the structure of the test is always the same.

The tasks

Part 1 consists of eight three-option multiple choice questions, each of which is based on a different monologue or conversation about 30 seconds long. Students hear each monologue or conversation twice. The question and options are read out on the tape as well as being printed in the question paper, so students are in no danger of losing their place. **Part 2** consists of a monologue or conversation, about three minutes long, with ten note-taking, sentence-completion or open-question items. Students are given time to read through the questions before the piece begins. The entire piece is repeated. Students are not penalised for minor spelling errors, providing their answers are recognisable as correct. **Part 3** consists of five short monologues or conversations, each about 30 seconds in length. There is a list of six possible answers which students must match against the pieces they hear. The group of five pieces is repeated. **Part 4** is usually a conversation, about three minutes in length. There are seven items, which may be three-option multiple choice or some other objectively marked type, such as True/False. They will not be note-taking items. There is time to read the items through before listening and the entire piece is repeated.

The Listening paper aims to test a range of skills, such as listening for gist and identifying the speaker, attitude or purpose. The format of **Part 1** allows students to have several 'fresh starts' so that they are less likely to feel discouraged in the early stages of the test. The fixed structure of the test is also designed to make students feel more secure in what is generally considered to be the most stressful part of the examination.

Preparing students

The best preparation for the Listening paper is exposure to a wide variety of spoken English. Students should be encouraged to listen to English in any form available, both in school and outside. For students who are not in an English-speaking country, information about English language broadcasts on the radio or television should be made available and students should be encouraged to seek out and share recorded material such as audio cassettes of pop songs and videos of films in English. It is not necessary for such material to use standard UK English. The important thing is for students to become habituated to listening to spoken English without a preamble in their mother tongue. In any case, some of the accents in the FCE examination are not standard UK, although they will never be very strong.

It is also essential for students to become thoroughly familiar with the format and aims of the Listening paper and to understand what is required in the different stages of the test. It is a good idea to introduce the Listening paper gradually by using one of the tests in this book simply to demonstrate what is required.

Students should also learn to use the printed questions as clues to what they will hear. Group discussion before listening will help to develop this skill. Teachers should bear in mind that these Practice Tests are at the level of difficulty of the examination and care should be taken not to undermine students' confidence by exposing them to the listening tasks under examination conditions too early.

Paper 5 Speaking

Format

The Speaking paper is designed to produce a sample of language from students which demonstrates their ability to give and exchange information and opinions. It lasts approximately 15 minutes and is divided into four parts in order to draw out different types of language.

Students are examined in pairs, allowing for a wide range of speaking skills to be sampled. There are also two examiners: an interlocutor, who conducts the test and contributes to assessment, and an assessor, who takes no part in the conversation, and is therefore free to concentrate entirely on assessing the students according to the FCE criteria.

The two examiners may exchange roles during the course of an examining session, but not during the examining of any one pair of students.

Note: The two candidates / two examiners interview format applies in almost all cases. Only in very exceptional circumstances may a small number of centres vary this by special arrangement with UCLES.

The tasks

The Speaking paper aims to sample a wide range of language, from simple social interaction to the more sophisticated exchanges required to solve problems, reach agreement or agree to differ, etc. Students should be encouraged to gain as much practical speaking experience as possible in order to build up their confidence in dealing with each part of the test. Each task requires the employment of a range of skills, and involves a slightly different type of interaction.

Part 1 (approximately four minutes) provides an opportunity for the two students to become accustomed to the examiners, each other and the examination situation while talking about familiar topics such as their personal background, interests, etc. Each student has a separate turn. This part of the paper tests mainly social language.

In **Part 2** (approximately four minutes), each student in turn is given two colour photos and is invited to talk about the photos and the related theme. Comments may be general or may relate to the student her/himself if appropriate. Some mention of the content of the photos will be appropriate, but this part should **not** be treated as an exercise in close description. This part of the paper tests the ability to convey information and express opinions.

In **Part 3** (approximately three minutes), the interlocutor gives the two students a visual stimulus (map, advertisements, photographs, etc.), which forms the basis of a joint task (prioritising, planning, decision-making, problem-solving, etc.). This task is on a different theme from **Part 2**. The students work on the task together, with the interlocutor offering only occasional guidance if required. This part of the paper requires the ability to negotiate and collaborate successfully in English, and tests the ability to exchange information and opinion, in conjunction with turn-taking and conversation management.

Part 4 (approximately four minutes), is an extension of **Part 3**, in which the students are invited by the interlocutor to discuss ideas related to the theme of **Part 3**. The interlocutor asks questions to facilitate a fruitful discussion. This part of the paper is an opportunity to extend and develop ideas from **Part 3** in a wider context, and tests the ability to formulate opinions and respond appropriately to those of the other student. Turn-taking again plays an important part.

Preparing students

PAIRWORK

Because the Speaking paper is conducted with pairs of students, it is normally relatively easy to incorporate examination practice into class activities.

For practical or pedagogical reasons, however, students in some learning situations may be unfamiliar with pairwork. In such cases, paired practice becomes particularly important, since students in this position, while quite happy to respond to their teacher in English, may find using the language to converse with their classmates artificial or even embarrassing. Such feelings are not conducive to making a good impression in the examination room. Equally, turn-taking and collaborative conversation are important features of the

Speaking paper. Students should practise these skills with each other, as they may not find it easy to question, interrupt or disagree with their teacher, even for the sake of practice.

If possible, it is also well worth working occasionally in threes or fours, with one student, or pair of students, acting as the examiner(s). Observing a pair in action, and having to manage the timing and the various tasks, can give a useful insight into what is expected in the examination.

GENERAL POINTS

The material for Paper 5 Part 2 in this book is organised thematically to facilitate concerted vocabulary and practice in the preparatory stages. The FCE examination itself may not have a thematic link in Part 2. Teachers who wish to reproduce full examination conditions in the later stages of their course, or for mock examination purposes, should simply combine the material from Tests 3 and 4 as follows:

For Test 3, use	3A and 3B with 4C and 4D	for Part 2;
	3E	for Part 3
For Test 4, use	4A and 4B with 3C and 3D	for Part 2;
	4E	for Part 3

Students should be encouraged to view the Speaking paper as an opportunity to demonstrate their ability, rather than a threat. The visual material is chosen to provide starting points for the development of productive exchanges between the participants, and not to catch students out on particular points of vocabulary or grammar. Tasks can, however, range across the 25 broad topic areas listed on page 3, and it is advisable for students to equip themselves with sufficient vocabulary to take part in a general conversation on any of these.

The practical side of taking part in the examination should not be neglected. A significant proportion of what a student says in the examination room is not governed by the themes of **Parts 2, 3** and **4**. Study, and regular practice, of the language required to introduce oneself, meet new people, express opinions, make suggestions, take turns, disagree politely, make a composed apology for errors, etc. will all help students to establish the core of a creditable performance. Students may need convincing, but skills like these are the real focus of the test, not the photographs and other material which serve as a vehicle for the Paper.

It is also useful to do some work on locating particular elements within the frame of a picture (*the man on the left, the house in the top left-hand corner*) or in relation to other elements in the picture (*the taller of the two women, the house opposite the cinema*). Pointing things out physically should be avoided.

It may be important to emphasise to some students that an item-by-item description of a photograph is not required by any of the tasks, and that such a description at this level is likely to be simple and repetitive in structure. It will also leave few openings for further discussion, a significant element in **Parts 2** and **4**, and for these reasons, it is unlikely to generate a good score on the Paper.

Teachers may wish to co-ordinate Speaking and Writing preparation, since both require the development of topic vocabulary. Simple additions to classwork (e.g., putting students in pairs to tell each other what they have written in their homework compositions and discuss any points arising) can be of tremendous benefit in mobilising recently acquired language. This type of activity should be kept short and to the point, and the importance of starting promptly should be emphasised. The timing of the Speaking paper is very tight, and it is important to avoid having thirty seconds' silence at the start of a three-minute task. Making students start quickly also encourages them to develop the skill of thinking 'on their feet' in English, which contributes greatly to taking a natural part in a fast-moving conversation.

Paper 5 frameworks

Test 1

Note: The colour pictures needed for Paper 5 appear on pages C1–12 in the Student's Book.

Part 1 (approximately four minutes)

Introduce yourself and the assessor.[*]
Encourage each candidate in turn to give personal information using questions such as:
   Where/What part of … are you from?
   How long have you lived here/there?
   Tell us what it's like living here/there …
If not in student's home town/country: What are the main differences between here and your home town/country?

Part 2 (approximately four minutes)

Tell the candidates what is going to happen:
   Now I'd like each of you to talk on your own for about a minute.
Say something like:
   I'm going to give each of you two different pictures and I'd like you to talk about them and say whether you'd like to study in this sort of place. (Candidate A), here are your two pictures. Please let (Candidate B) see them. They show different places where you might study.
Indicate the pictures 1A and 1B to Candidate A. Say:
   (Candidate B), I'll give you your two pictures in a moment.
Then invite Candidate A to begin, by saying, for example:
   (Candidate A), I'd like you to compare and contrast these pictures, saying how you'd feel about studying in such places. Remember, you have only about a minute for this, so don't worry if I interrupt you. All right?
Candidate A speaks for approximately one minute.
Thank Candidate A, retrieve the pictures and invite Candidate B to speak:
   (Candidate B), could you tell us which of those places you would prefer to study in?
Candidate B speaks for approximately 20 seconds.
   Thank you. Now, (Candidate B), here are your pictures. Please let (Candidate A) see them. They show some other places to study.

---

[*] The assessor may not of course be present when students are practising with their teacher, but they should become accustomed to the idea that there will be a second examiner in the room who does not join in their conversation (see p. 12).

Indicate the pictures 1C and 1D to Candidate B. Say something like:
(Candidate B), I'd like you to compare and contrast these study environments and say whether you prefer one of them. Do you ever study in places like these? Remember, you have only about a minute for this, so don't worry if I interrupt you. All right?
Candidate B speaks for approximately one minute.
Thank Candidate B.
Retrieve the pictures and say something like:
(Candidate A), could you tell us which of those places you'd prefer to study in?
Candidate A speaks for approximately 20 seconds.
Thank the candidates and move on to Part 3.

Part 3 (approximately three minutes)

Say:
Now, I'd like you to do something together.
Indicate the town plan (1E) to both candidates. Ask them to consider which of the three locations A, B, or C would be the best site for a new hospital. Say:
Here is a plan of part of a town. You can see three areas marked A, B and C. The town is going to have a new hospital. I'd like you to talk together and decide which of the areas marked would be best and why. It is not necessary to agree with each other. All right? You have only about three minutes for this, so, once again, don't worry if I stop you and please speak so that we can hear you.
If the candidates are having difficulty keeping the conversation going, it may be necessary to support them with an extra question or remark, but it is important to avoid stepping in too soon.
After about three minutes thank the candidates and move on to Part 4.

Part 4 (approximately four minutes)

Encourage the candidates to develop topics raised by their discussion in Part 3.
Depending on the way their discussion went, possible questions might be:
Are cities too noisy?
What can be done to reduce noise pollution in cities?

How important is it that there should be good public transport?
Do people use private cars too much? Why?
Do you think the traffic in cities should be controlled more strictly? How?

Is it important for local people to be involved in planning decisions? Why?
Are local people sufficiently involved in planning decisions on the whole?
If not, why not? What could be done to improve this?

Test 2

Note: The colour pictures needed for Paper 5 appear on pages C1–12 in the Student's Book.

Part 1 (approximately four minutes)

Introduce yourself and the assessor. *
Encourage each candidate in turn to give personal information using questions such as:
> Do you have brothers and sisters? Tell me something about them …
> Do you get on well together?
> What are the advantages/disadvantages of being an only child/a member of a large family?
> Do you see much of the older members of your family? Your grandparents, for example?

Part 2 (approximately four minutes)

Tell the candidates what is going to happen:
> Now I'd like each of you to talk on your own for about a minute.

Say something like:
> I'm going to give each of you two different pictures and I'd like you to talk about them and say whether you like to eat in this sort of place.
> (Candidate A), here are your two pictures. Please let (Candidate B) see them. They show different places where you might eat.

Indicate the pictures 2A and 2B to Candidate A. Say:
> (Candidate B), I'll give you your two pictures in a moment.

Then invite Candidate A to begin, by saying, for example:
> (Candidate A), I'd like you to compare and contrast these pictures, saying how you'd feel about eating in such places. Remember, you have only about a minute for this, so don't worry if I interrupt you. All right?

Candidate A speaks for approximately one minute.

Thank Candidate A, retrieve the pictures and invite Candidate B to speak:
> (Candidate B), could you tell us which of those places you would prefer to eat in?

Candidate B speaks for approximately 20 seconds.
> Thank you. Now, (Candidate B), here are your pictures. Please let (Candidate A) see them. They show some other places to eat.

Indicate the pictures 2C and 2D to Candidate B. Say something like:
> (Candidate B), I'd like you to compare and contrast these places and say whether you prefer one of them? Do you ever eat in places like these? Remember, you have only about a minute for this, so don't worry if I interrupt you. All right?

Candidate B speaks for approximately one minute.

---

* The assessor may not of course be present when students are practising with their teacher, but they should become accustomed to the idea that there will be a second examiner in the room who does not join in their conversation (see p. 12).

Thank Candidate B.
Retrieve the pictures and say something like:
    (Candidate A), could you tell us which of these places you'd prefer to eat in?
Candidate A speaks for approximately 20 seconds.
Thank the candidates and move on to Part 3.

Part 3 (approximately three minutes)

Say:
    Now, I'd like you to do something together.
Indicate the presents (2E) and the pictures of people (2F) to both candidates.
Ask them to decide which of the presents would be most suitable for each of their 'friends'. Say:
    Here are some presents you might buy in Britain to take to friends abroad.
    Here are four people you want to choose presents for. I'd like you to talk
    together and decide which present would be best for each person and why. It
    is not necessary to agree with each other. All right? You have only about
    three minutes for this, so, once again, don't worry if I stop you and please
    speak so that we can hear you.
*If the candidates are having difficulty keeping the conversation going, it may be
necessary to support them with an extra question or remark, but it is important
to avoid stepping in too soon.*
After about three minutes thank the candidates and move on to Part 4.

Part 4 (approximately four minutes)

Encourage the candidates to develop topics raised by their discussion in Part 3.
Depending on the way their discussion went, possible questions might be:
    Do you enjoy giving people presents? Why/Why not?
    How do you decide what to give?

    When do people give presents in your country?
    For birthdays, special occasions …?
    What sort of things do they give?
    Are there any traditions in your country about giving or receiving presents?
    For example, should you open a present immediately when you are given it?
    Why/Why not?

    Do people spend too much money on unnecessary things nowadays, things
    like tourist souvenirs …?

    What sort of things do people buy as souvenirs from your country?
    Do you think these are the right sort of things for them to buy?

Test 3

Note: The colour pictures needed for Paper 5 appear on pages C1–12 in the Student's Book.

Part 1 (approximately four minutes)

*Introduce yourself and the assessor.**
Encourage each candidate in turn to give personal information using questions such as:

What do you enjoy doing in your free time?
Tell me a bit about what you actually do when you …
How long have you been interested in …?
Can you explain something about the rules of …/why people enjoy …/the attraction of …?

Part 2 (approximately four minutes)

Tell the candidates what is going to happen:

Now I'd like each of you to talk on your own for about a minute.
Say something like:

I'm going to give each of you two different pictures and I'd like you to talk about them and say whether you'd like to travel this way.
(Candidate A), here are your two pictures. Please let (Candidate B) see them. They show different ways of travelling.
Indicate the pictures 3A and 3B to Candidate A. Say:

(Candidate B), I'll give you your two pictures in a moment.
Then invite Candidate A to begin, by saying, for example:

(Candidate A), I'd like you to compare and contrast these pictures, saying how you'd feel about travelling like this. Remember, you have only about a minute for this, so don't worry if I interrupt you. All right?
Candidate A speaks for approximately one minute.
Thank Candidate A, retrieve pictures and invite Candidate B to speak:

(Candidate B),could you tell us which of those ways of travelling you would prefer?
Candidate B speaks for approximately 20 seconds.

Thank you. Now, (Candidate B), here are your pictures. Please let (Candidate A) see them. They show some other ways of travelling.
Indicate the pictures 3C and 3D to Candidate B. Say something like:

(Candidate B), I'd like you to compare and contrast these ways of travelling and say whether you prefer one of them. Have you ever travelled like this? Remember, you have only about a minute for this, so don't worry if I interrupt you. All right?
Candidate B speaks for approximately one minute.
Thank Candidate B.

---

* The assessor may not of course be present when students are practising with their teacher, but they should become accustomed to the idea that there will be a second examiner in the room who does not join in their conversation (see p. 12).

Retrieve the pictures and say something like:
   (Candidate A), could you tell us which of those ways you'd prefer to travel?
Candidate A speaks for approximately 20 seconds.
Thank the candidates and move on to Part 3.

Part 3 (approximately three minutes)

Say:
   Now, I'd like you to do something together.
Indicate the illustration 'Success in Sport' (3E) to both candidates. Ask them to consider which of the reasons given are most important in deciding whether people are successful in sport. Say:
   Here are some reasons why people succeed in sport. I'd like you to talk
   together and decide which are the most important and which don't matter so
   much. It is not necessary to agree with each other. All right? You have only
   about three minutes for this, so, once again, don't worry if I stop you and
   please speak so that we can hear you.
If the candidates are having difficulty keeping the conversation going, it may be necessary to support them with an extra question or remark, but it is important to avoid stepping in too soon.
After about three minutes thank the candidates and move on to Part 4.

Part 4 (approximately four minutes)

Encourage the candidates to develop topics raised by their discussion in Part 3.
Depending on the way their discussion went, possible questions might be:
   Is it better to watch sport on television or live?
   Are famous sports people good models for young people to follow?
   Why/Why not?
   What dangers are involved in international sport?
   Is there too much advertising in sport?
   Do people attach too much importance to sports nowadays? Why/Why not?

   What could be done to help young sportsmen and women in your area?
   Should governments give more support to young sportsmen and women?
   Why/Why not?

Test 4

Note: The colour pictures needed for Paper 5 appear on pages C1–12 in the
Student's Book.

Part 1 (approximately four minutes)

*Introduce yourself and the assessor.**

* The assessor may not of course be present when students are practising with their teacher,
  but they should become accustomed to the idea that there will be a second examiner in the
  room who does not join in their conversation (see p. 12).

Encourage each candidate in turn to give personal information using questions such as:

Are you studying English for any special purpose?
In what way do you think English will be useful to you in the future?
If not, why not?
What other languages do you/would you like to study? Why?
Can you tell me about your career plans?

For candidates still at school: What will you do when you leave school?

Part 2 (approximately four minutes)

Tell the candidates what is going to happen:

Now I'd like each of you to talk on your own for about a minute.

Say something like:

I'm going to give each of you two different pictures of houses and I'd like you to talk about them and say what you think it would be like to live in these places.
(Candidate A), here are your two pictures. Please let (Candidate B) see them. They show different houses.

Indicate the pictures 4A and 4B to Candidate A. Say:

(Candidate B), I'll give you your two pictures in a moment.

Then invite Candidate A to begin, by saying, for example:

(Candidate A), I'd like you to compare and contrast these pictures, saying how you'd feel about living in such places. Remember, you only have about a minute for this, so don't worry if I interrupt you. All right?

Candidate A speaks for approximately one minute.

Thank Candidate A, retrieve the pictures and invite Candidate B to speak:

(Candidate B), could you tell us which of those places you would prefer to live in?

Candidate B speaks for approximately 20 seconds.

Thank you. Now, (Candidate B), here are your pictures. Please let (Candidate A) see them. They show some other houses.

Indicate the pictures 4C and 4D to Candidate B. Say something like:

(Candidate B), I'd like you to compare and contrast these houses and say whether you prefer one of them. Have you ever lived in places like these? Remember, you have only about a minute for this so don't worry if I interrupt you. All right?

Candidate B speaks for approximately one minute.

Thank Candidate B.

Retrieve the pictures and say something like:

(Candidate A), could you tell us which of those places you'd prefer to live in?

Candidate A speaks for approximately 20 seconds.

Thank the candidates and move on to Part 3.

Part 3 (approximately three minutes)

Say:

Now, I'd like you to do something together.

Indicate the photograph 4E to both candidates. Tell them that this is someone

who is going for a job interview and needs some advice. Ask them to discuss
what they should tell her. Say:

> Here is a young woman who wants to get a job looking after elderly people.
> She's going for her interview tomorrow and she wants your advice about her
> appearance. I'd like you to talk together and discuss whether she should
> change her appearance, and if so, how. It is not necessary to agree with each
> other. All right? You have only about three minutes for this, so, once again,
> don't worry if I stop you and please speak so that we can hear you.

If the candidates are having difficulty keeping the conversation going, it may be
necessary to support them with an extra question or remark, but it is important
to avoid stepping in too soon.

After about three minutes thank the candidates and move on to Part 4.

Part 4 (approximately four minutes)

Encourage the candidates to develop topics raised by their discussion in Part 3.
Depending on the way their discussion went, possible questions might be:

> Do you think it's important to dress smartly for work?
> Have you ever had problems with your teachers or parents about the clothes
> you wear?
> Why do some young people wear very unusual clothes?
> Do people's clothes tell you about their personalities?
> How much do you care about being in fashion?
> Are fashion clothes good value for money?
> Do fashions have too much influence on what people buy?

Recording answers

Paper 1, Paper 3 and Paper 4

Answers for these papers are recorded on computerised answer sheets which are marked by OMR (Optical Mark Reader). Samples are given in the Student's Book and these may be photocopied without further permission. Teachers are strongly advised to encourage the use of these sheets whenever possible, so that students are not troubled or distracted during the actual examination by the mechanics of recording their answers.

Paper 1

For this paper, students shade in lozenges in pencil to indicate their answers, A, B, C etc. These pencil marks are read by the OMR. It is important that students use soft pencil as the OMR is not sensitive to ink. If a mistake is made, students should carefully erase the mark with a rubber. Correcting fluid should not be used.

It is better for students to answer directly onto the OMR sheet rather than copy answers at the end to avoid making copying errors under pressure of time. Particular care should be taken not to record answers against the wrong question numbers, for example when leaving an answer blank. If any questions remain unanswered at the end, it is better to fill in a guess than to leave a blank.

Part 4 may include questions which require two or more answers. These may be given in any order.

Paper 3 and Paper 4

Although these papers are marked by hand, OMR sheets are used to speed up processing and ensure accuracy of addition. Some parts (Paper 3 Part 1, Paper 4 Parts 1 and 3) require students to shade in lozenges in pencil, as for Paper 1. The other parts require students to write in an answer. For these, students should write clearly, preferably in ink, in the spaces provided. Errors with shaded lozenges should be carefully erased, as for Paper 1. Where correction of a written answer on the OMR is unavoidable, a single line through the incorrect word(s) is quite sufficient; there is no need to 'block out' mistakes and correcting fluid should not be used. Students with particularly large hand-writing may need practice in moderating their style to deal comfortably with the answer sheet. If blanks remain at the end of the paper, it is better to guess than to leave a question unanswered.

For **Paper 3** students should be advised to answer directly onto the answer sheet, to avoid copying errors, as accuracy is very important. The required answers to the five parts take the following forms:

Part 1 Shade in the lozenge of the correct option A, B, C or D in pencil.
Part 2 Write **one word only** (preferably in ink).

Part 3 Write between **two** and **five** words (preferably in ink).
Part 4 Tick (✓) correct lines; write **one word only** for incorrect lines (preferably in ink).
Paper 5 Write one word only (preferably in ink).

For **Paper 4,** time is allowed at the end of the paper for transfer of answers, so students should write on the question paper and ignore the OMR until the last five minutes.

The required answers to the five parts take the following forms:
Part 1 Shade in the lozenge of the correct option A, B, or C in pencil.
Part 2 Write a word or short phrase (preferably in ink). Complete sentences are never required.
Part 3 Shade in the lozenge of the correct option A, B, C, D, E or F in pencil.
Part 4 Write the letter of the correct option (preferably in ink). These may vary from test to test.

Paper 2

Answers should be written in ink in the spaces provided on the question paper. The question number, but not the question, should be written at the beginning of the answer to Part 2. Organisation of content is assessed, so attention should be paid to punctuation, and paragraphing should be clear. No particular formats are expected, however. The report, for example, need not follow the conventions of formal business style. Although legibility is not assessed as such, work which is difficult to read will not improve students' chances of a good mark.

Careful planning of answers will help students to avoid messy and disorganised work. Where amendments are necessary, they should be made as neatly as possible, indicating material which is to be ignored by crossing out with a single line *not* by using brackets.

Marking and grading

General procedures

All five papers of the FCE examination carry equal weighting. Each of the five papers is marked out of a different total, but the scores are weighted by computer so that each paper contributes 20 per cent to the total mark.

Each paper is marked in a slightly different way. Samples of OMR answer sheets for Papers 1, 3 and 4 appear at the back of the Student's Book.

The Reading paper is marked by an optical mark reader (OMR). The OMR sheets are scanned by the reader which is programmed with the correct keys.

The Writing paper is marked by EFL examiners who are trained and monitored through a co-ordination process.

The Use of English paper is marked by a combination of clerical marking and OMR. **Part 1** is marked by an OMR as for the Reading paper. The other parts have a tightly controlled mark-scheme which allows for clerical marking.

The Listening paper is marked by a combination of clerical marking and OMR. **Parts 1** and **3** are marked by an OMR. The other parts are clerically marked according to a tightly controlled mark-scheme.

The Speaking paper is assessed by two examiners.

The scores on the five components are added together by a computer after scaling. The final 'aggregate' mark determines the candidate's grade.

Results slip

Each candidate receives a results slip which tells them what grade they have achieved. This is in the range from A through to E plus U. A, B and C are passing grades; D, E and U are failing grades; U is unclassified. Candidates who fail are given an indication of the papers in which their performance was very weak, while candidates who pass are told which papers they did really well in.

Assessment and marking of Paper 2

Successful FCE candidates will typically meet the following requirements in the Writing paper:
• The demands of the task should be achieved within the word limits, and all the main points should be covered.

- Awareness of the appropriate register for the task should be demonstrated and maintained.
- The text should be suitably set out using appropriate paragraphing and the ideas should be clearly linked.
- The range of structure and vocabulary should be adequate to fulfil the requirements of the task.
- Any errors of structure or vocabulary should not impede communication.
- Handwriting should be legible.
- The text should have a satisfactory effect on the target reader.

The most able candidates will typically produce a wide range of structures and vocabulary, making few errors in spelling and punctuation. Their answers will include relevant and possibly some original details. The text would have a positive or very positive effect on the reader.

Candidates who are below FCE standard are likely to demonstrate many of the following weaknesses in the Writing paper: use of a very limited range of structure and vocabulary; failure to meet all the requirements of the task; omission of relevant points; inappropriate lifting from the questions; inclusion of irrelevant material; number of words either far below 120 or well above 180; poor lay-out or organisation; little or no use of linking devices; lack of awareness of appropriate register. Their writing does not clearly communicate the message to the target reader and may therefore have a negative effect.

Sample answers

The following pieces of writing have been selected from students' answers produced during trialling. In order to help teachers in assessing the work of their own students, marks out of a possible total of 20 have been awarded based on the assessment criteria for the examination. Explanatory notes have been added to show how these marks have been arrived at. In this scoring system, successful candidates should normally expect to score 11 and above out of 20.

Sample answer A

Question answered:	Test 2 Part2 Question 2
Mark:	18 out of 20
Comments:	Good appreciation of the task set with well-conceived execution. Varied and generally well-expressed ideas with some successful attempts at more sophisticated language. Few errors, appropriate register and good control of complex structures.
Length:	154 words

Some weeks ago, I saw a film with the actor Tom Hanks. The film is called "Forest Gump" and I really enjoyed it. It's about the life of a person whose name is Forest Gump. Gump is not very intelligent and he has been teased by other people during his whole life. However, he has always had luck and in the end, he becomes very popular even though he didn't do anything for being famous.

From my point of view, the actor Tom Hanks plays his part excellently. You really must love the character he plays. Although Gump is a dull person who doesn't understand what occurs around him, he's always in the centre of events.

Personally I liked this film very much because it gives evidence of the society in general. You must read between the line. If you're not able to look in depth you will think the film is just silly.

Sample answer B

Question answered: Test 3 Part 1 Question 1

Mark: 16 out of 20

Comments: Successful handling of the task with information well selected and integrated. Varied sentence structure and generally accurate grammar, presenting no major problems for the reader.

Length: 179 words

Dear Paul,

I'm writing to give you some news about the holiday I'm spending in Greece.

Since I arrived nine days ago, I've done all sorts of things, like sports, sightseeing tours, and going to a disco or a cinema in the evening. One exciting experience was sailing for the first time in my life. I know you enjoy doing that sport, so this is one reason I think it would be nice to come back together next year.

If the weather doesn't permit to go on the beach, I can have a swim in one of the pools belonging to the hotel; there are a lot of young people doing the same things and it's easy to get to know them. Also the family who run the hotel are very friendly and the food is quite good.

I can't write now about all the activities provided; I'll tell you about them when I get back next week, and I hope to persuade you to share this experience next time.

I look forward to seeing you soon,

Bye,

xxxx

Sample answer C

Question answered:	Test 3 Part 1 Question 1
Mark:	15 out of 20
Comments:	Generally clear, but with a consistent level of minor error. Task competently handled but with little attempt at development.
Length:	176 words

Dear Sandra,

I'm now on holiday at the Bayview Hotel. Everything is wonderful and I've a really good time. The hotel is all I need; a restaurant with delicious food, bar and two pools.

As soon as I arrived to the Bayview I decided to come back next year and I would like you to come with me. We could have so much fun together here. It's a cinema, discos and a lot of shops near the hotel and we can always go for a walk in the mountains or try sailing. Tomorrow I'm going to sail, it's the first time for me and I'm looking foreward to it.

Apart from that, the hotel organize trips every day to interesting places. On Tuesday I'm going by coach to the old town and a museum.

Finally the best thing is that the hotel is very cheap so why don't you come with me? Think about it and tell me your decision next month.

I'm looking foreward to hearing from you!

             Love,

                XXXX

Sample answer D

Question answered: Test 3 Part 2 Question 4

Mark: 13 out of 20

Comments: Reasonable treatment of task. Regular errors, some of which might cause problems for non-specialist readers, but most ideas clearly communicated. Simple, repetitive sentence structure.

Length: 171 words

One evening I went with my husband to the local restaurant near where we lives. It's an Italian restaurant, there you can eat lots of pizza and pasta. We can't complain about the food, because we had a lovely dinner. There were plenty of dishes you could choose between. and it wasn't so expensive either. the restaurant it selves is very nice and the atmosphere is very pleased. There are always lot's of customers and the waiters are all the time busy. "That was the problem". It took an hour before we could order and we had to wait a long time before we got the bill. Meanwhile the waiters looked like they were going to get a heart attack. I and my husband felt very sorry for them. So we didn't want to make a complaint.

In conclusion we recommend it for you who have time to wait, because the dinner is splended.

The restaurant is named Roma and is situated on Hannover Street.

We hope you enjoy your food.

Sample answer E

Question answered:	Test 4 Part 1 Question 1
Mark:	11 out of 20
Comments:	Overlong, largely due to preoccupation with detailed directions. Register deteriorates steadily from good tone in first paragraph to very casual last sentence. Some basic errors, but does achieve task.
Length:	226 words

Dear Mr John Stevens,

I'm writing to confirm my invite to the Swansea College to talk about "The Industrial Revolution in South Wales" – I'm sorry to tell you that it's impossible for me to meet your train because it arrives at 16.45 and I'm busy until 17.00. Apologising for not being able to take you at the station, I would like to suggest you the different ways to arrive at the School, so that you can choose the best.

If you prefer going on foot, this is possible because the School is not so far from the station: you could go down High Street and take the first turning on the right and then go straight on Alexandra Road – you'll pass the library on the left At the first corner on the right you'll find the Fire Station, turn there and go straight ahead until you get to the School on the right – Another possibilty is taking a bus: the bus stop is in front of the Station and you can get off the bus at the Mount Pleasant Hospital; then you can go back on the same street on foot until you can see the School on your left.

If you are tired or in late, you could take a taxi on High Street only a few metres far from the station.

Yours, faithfully
XXXX

Sample Answer F

Question answered: Test 4 Part 2 Question 2

Mark: 7 out of 20

Comments: Nature of task entirely misunderstood: by presenting a whole meal, the candidate effectively minimises the opportunity for *instructional* language, which is the intended task focus. Consistent level of basic error. Overuse of non-English terms with little attempt to explain or contextualise.

Length: 205 words

Dear Patty

Thank you for your last letter. I'm very interested in your idea about having a traditional lunch of my country for celebrate your friend's birthday. I'm writing for giving you some advice.

I'm sure you are a small group of people, so you will have a good result. the meal that I have chosen is very simple, but remember to take care carefully at the preparation of the receipeits.

I suggest you to start with several "crostini" with jam like appetizers, then go on with "spaghetti al pomodoro". You ought to cook the tomatoes with garlic in oil just only few minutes and add some bazil at the end. As regards the main course you should prepare "melanzane alla parmigiana" with roasted pork steak. the slices of vegetables have been cooked in a pan put in the oven with the slices of "mozzarella" and grated "parmigiano" for us! As for cakes is concerned you ought to prepare an apple cake.

I hope you're satisfied with my instructions. I'm sure that if you follow me my advice your guest will keen on the meal.

As soon as possible, give me the news about you and obviously how the lunch's gone

With my best wishes from
XXXXX

Sample answer G

Question answered:	Test 3 Part 2 Question 4
Mark:	4 out of 20
Comments:	Task entirely misunderstood, resulting in first person narrative, where a more general report is called for. Consistently poor control of grammar and sentence structure. Communication breaks down completely towards end.
Length:	124 words

A local newspaper invited some readers for lunch in a local restaurant. I was one of them and I decided to go.

We arrived at the restaurant it was outside from the city and it was quite small. I was simply but the atmosphere was very friendly. I had a fine place the tables were round and it had vase with flowers on them. The staff welcome us and serviced. The food was excellent Except an event which happened. One of the waiter when he served fall down a glass of wine on me, when the boss of the restaurant saw that came near he told to him in front of us You're fired.

It was very rude to fire an employee like this.

Assessment and marking of Paper 5

Candidates are assessed according to the following criteria:
- Linguistic resource (including control of appropriate structures and the use of varied and appropriate vocabulary)
- Pronunciation of sentences, words and individual sounds (for example, rhythm and intonation patterns, stressed and unstressed sounds)
- Fluency (speed and rhythm, choice of structures, general naturalness and clarity)
- Interactive communication (for example, turn-taking, holding the floor, negotiating meaning, initiating and responding)
- Task achievement (that is, treatment of the task in terms of coherence, organisation of main points and appropriateness of language).

Successful FCE candidates will typically meet the following requirements in the Speaking paper:
- sufficient range and control of structures to deal adequately with the task
- adequate range and control of vocabulary to talk about subjects of general interest and to achieve the task
- pronunciation foreign but enough control over pronunciation of individual sounds, stress-timing, rhythm, and placing of stress and intonation in words and sentences to achieve broad understanding
- discussion of the task without so much hesitation that communication is impeded
- sufficient sensitivity to turn-taking, ability to initiate discussion and respond to questions, negotiate and elaborate meaning where required.

The most able candidates will typically have control over a wide range of structures with few gaps in vocabulary for everyday situations; pronunciation may be foreign-sounding but very easily understood; natural hesitation; full and natural contribution to the interaction with occasional minor difficulties in turn-taking or negotiation; effective, comprehensive and independent treatment of the task.

Candidates who are below FCE standard are likely to demonstrate many of the following features: inaccurate use of structures; insufficient range and inaccurate use of vocabulary; pronunciation which makes them difficult to understand; unacceptable hesitation which strains the listener; difficulty in contributing to and maintaining a discussion; inadequate or irrelevant attempts at the task requiring too much redirection or assistance.

Test 1 Key

Paper 1 Reading

Part 1
1 C   2 F   3 H   4 A   5 G   6 E   7 B

Part 2
8 B   9 D   10 A   11 B   12 D   13 B   14 A   15 C

Part 3
16 B   17 D   18 G   19 E   20 A   21 C

Part 4
22 and 23 A/C   24 B   25 C   26 F   27 and 28 D/H   29 D
30 G   31 C   32 A   33 and 34 E/G   35 H
(Where there are two possible answers, these are interchangeable.)

Paper 3 Use of English

Award one mark for each correct answer, except in Part 3, where two marks are available, divided up as shown, for each answer.
    Correct spelling is essential throughout. Ignore omission or abuse of capital letters. No half marks.

Part 1
1 B   2 A   3 C   4 D   5 A   6 D   7 D   8 B
9 C   10 A   11 D   12 C   13 B   14 A   15 A

Part 2
16 where   17 how   18 anyone/anybody   19 tried/attempted/threatened
20 after   21 no   22 a/per/each/every   23 The   24 whose
25 yet/but/(al)though   26 of   27 as   28 If/Provided/Providing
29 to   30 will/can

Part 3
31 accused Frank of (1) breaking/having broken (1)
32 must have/get (1) my car (1)
33 wishes she (1) had bought (1)
34 if you (1) hadn't/had not helped (1) OR but for/without you/your (1) helping (1)
35 in case (1) I ran (1)
36 have fallen (1) through (1)

37 wasn't/was not (1) fresh enough (1)
38 may have (1) gone (1)
39 is/'s impossible (1) for me to (1)
40 was (1) being watched (1)

Part 4

41 much   42 until   43 ✓   44 it   45 myself   46 one
47 ✓   48 ✓   49 out   50 to   51 ✓   52 with   53 so
54 all   55 for

Part 5

56 life   57 noticing   58 originally   59 convenience   60 sale
61 widened   62 shorter   63 underground   64 likelihood
65 freedom

Paper 4 Listening

Part 1

1 B   2 C   3 B   4 A   5 B   6 A   7 B   8 A

Part 2

9 useful for future/helpful for career/wants to be a nurse *etc.*
10 farmhouse   11 road   12 lifts   13 (taking round) evening drinks
14 money/costs *etc.*   15 grateful (for extras)   16 her son-in-law
17 (an) equal/(just) the same (as them)   18 organise (a) concert

Part 3

19 B   20 A   21 C   22 F   23 E

Part 4

24 T   25 T   26 T   27 F   28 T   29 F   30 F

Transcript   *First Certificate Practice Test One. Paper Four. Listening. Hello, I'm going to give you the instructions for this test. I'll introduce each part of the test and give you time to look at the questions. At the start of each piece, you'll hear this sound:*

tone

You'll hear each piece twice.

Remember, while you're listening, write your answers on the question paper. You'll have time at the end of the test to copy your answers onto the separate answer sheet.
The tape will now be stopped. Please ask any questions now, because you must not speak during the test.

[pause]

PART 1 *Now, open your question paper and look at Part One.*
You'll hear people talking in eight different situations. For questions 1 to 8,
choose the best answer, A, B or C.

Question 1 *One*
You are visiting a museum when you hear this man addressing a group of
people. Who is he?
A a security guard
B a tourist guide
C a museum guide

[pause]

tone

Tourist guide: O.K. everyone, uh, before we go into the next room I'd like to warn you not to try and touch any of the wall-hangings or furniture. As you will see they're very beautiful, with very delicate finishes. The museum is very strict about this and they will ask you to leave if they think you're not taking the rule seriously. I actually had someone told to leave when I brought a group here last year because he accidentally brushed against something. Um?

[pause]

tone

[The recording is repeated.]

[pause]

Question 2 *Two*
You're in a restaurant when you overhear one of the waiters talking. Who is
he talking about?
A a colleague
B the manager
C a customer

[pause]

tone

Waiter: Well, I said, I don't stand for that sort of thing from anyone. I don't care whether they've been coming here since before I was born, they've no right to speak to anyone like that. I'm doing my job and it's my job to serve her a meal, not run up and down the road with messages. She's going to complain about me she said. Well, I'm going to complain about her!

[pause]

tone

[The recording is repeated.]

[pause]

Question 3

Three
You're waiting in a hospital corridor when you hear this woman talking.
What does she say about her doctor?
A He's made a mistake.
B He's been unhelpful.
C He's been untruthful.

[pause]

tone

Woman: To be honest I thought at first he'd got my notes mixed up with someone else. We didn't seem to be talking about the same illness. He kept going on about how it's not uncommon for these side-effects to occur. And I thought, that's all very well for you to say, but I'm the only case I know, and I asked what he was going to do now. Well, he just sort of smiled, and said something about 'weighing discomfort against disease', really pompous! And that was it as far as he was concerned.

[pause]

tone

[The recording is repeated.]

[pause]

Question 4

Four
You are out shopping when you hear a shop assistant talking to a customer.
What is she refusing to do?
A give him some money
B change a faulty item
C repair something

[pause]

tone

Shop assistant: Unfortunately, it's just not possible for me to do that. I don't have the authority, you see.
Man: But, but, it's faulty. I know my rights.
Shop assistant: But I can't tell if there's really anything wrong with it, just looking at it, so the best I can do is give you a credit note as if you'd changed your mind about wanting it. Then you can choose goods to the same value, well, either now or at a later date. Because we don't give cash refunds unless there's something actually wrong with the item. Otherwise, I can have it sent back for checking, but I still can't pay anything out till we've had confirmation of a fault.

[pause]

tone

[The recording is repeated.]

[pause]

Question 5 *Five*
Listen to this woman introducing the next speaker at a conference. Why has she been asked to introduce him?
A He is an old friend.
B He is a former student of hers.
C He is a colleague.

[pause]

tone

Conference chair: Now, it gives me the greatest pleasure to introduce our keynote speaker. I take no small pride in having had even a minor role in the development of one of the most forward-thinking workers in his field. We shared many fascinating discussions as he raced through my course, too many years ago now. I can hardly claim to have taught, merely to have helped along the way, although he has been kind enough to say he learnt from me! Anyway, I'm very honoured to present to you ….

[pause]

tone

[The recording is repeated.]

[pause]

Question 6 *Six*
You are staying in a farmhouse when you hear your host on the telephone. Who is he talking to?
A a supplier
B a customer
C an employee

[pause]

tone

Farmer: No, no, I'm sorry, I simply can't accept that. I'm running a business here, too, and I can't just turn round and tell my customers that, well, sorry, no vegetables this week, I haven't had time to pick them! I've got fields here waiting to be planted out. You've been telling me for a week you'd have the fertiliser in stock tomorrow. I need it on that field today. If you can't get it here I'll have to find someone else who can.

[pause]

tone

[The recording is repeated.]

[pause]

Question 7   Seven
You hear this critic talking on the radio. What is she recommending?
A   a film
B   a book
C   an exhibition

[pause]

tone

Critic: I was really pleased to be asked to review this, because I was enormously curious to see whether Delaney could handle the change of medium, whether he could colour in the bits between the dialogue, so to speak. In fact I think he's done very well, and there's no sign of that horrid 'book of the film' feel that you sometimes get from people who are crossing over from script-writing to the novel. The characters are very finely drawn and right from the first chapter the plot is cleverly worked. I have some little doubts about …

[pause]

tone

[The recording is repeated.]

[pause]

Question 8   Eight
You are walking up the street when you hear this man talking to a woman at her front door. What does he want to do?
A   interview her
B   help her
C   advise her

[pause]

tone

Reporter: I won't keep you more than a few minutes, and I'm sure if you think about it, you'll realise that talking to someone like me will be a lot better than leaving people to make everything up. Because I can assure you, they will make it up, if you don't get your story out first, so why not just give me your side of things now?

[pause]

tone

[The recording is repeated.]

[pause]

That's the end of Part One.
Now turn to Part Two.

PART 2   *You will hear a student called Bill talking about his holiday job. For questions 9 to 18, complete the notes which summarise what he says. You will need to write a word or a short phrase. You now have forty-five seconds in which to look at Part Two.*

[pause]

tone

Bill: Yeah, over last summer I did this job in an old people's home. I'd been looking for work and I said I wanted something which might be useful, because I want to train as a nurse when I finish school, so they said what about a care assistant, and I said, sure. So, anyway, I went along and it's in this old house, it was a farmhouse, but the farm's all gone, now the town's got bigger, and it's just got a bit of a garden round it. It's got a lawn and flowerbeds at the back, but the front is quite near the road. I was surprised but the old people like it they say, because they can watch what's going on a bit. You know, some places, they're very pretty, but so quiet and they feel cut off. It's quite a nice building, with lots of the old woodwork and so on, just they've put in a couple of lifts for obvious reasons, because they've got some quite frail people among the residents.

I really liked the work, which was a relief, and I got on pretty well with most of the residents. Some of them were a good laugh. They like talking about when they were younger. The best part of my work was when I'd take round their evening drinks, I wouldn't be having to rush off, and I could take time to listen. I suppose they'd told all their stories before but I hadn't heard them, so I was a good audience.

I didn't see much of Mrs Stone, that's the owner, but she seemed all right. She's got two or three of these places, and I think she's always concerned about whether she's going to lose money. But I don't think she's mean. She just can't afford not to be businesslike about it, or they'd go bust. The residents mostly seemed to like her, anyway. They were nice, most of them, one or two of the old girls could be a bit snappy, but I think that was their arthritis, and the old boys were all ever so grateful if you had time to do them any little extras. The only really tricky one was this old girl who thought I was her son-in-law, because of my hair being the same colour, and she didn't get on with her son-in-law, so she didn't get on with me. But I survived, anyway. The rest of the staff did what they could. It was really good, being treated just the same, like an equal, by very experienced people. It made me value my own work and try to do it as well as them. It was a really useful experience, and I learnt a lot. I'm going back there next month, because I'm organising a concert for them. They're looking forward to it. And what I wanted to ask, was whether anyone …

[pause]

tone

Now you'll hear Part Two again.

[The recording is repeated.]

[pause]

That's the end of Part Two.
Now turn to Part Three.

PART 3   *You will hear five different women talking about parties.*
For questions 19 to 23, choose from the list A to F what they describe. Use
the letters only once. There is one extra letter which you do not need to use.
You now have 30 seconds in which to look at Part Three.

[pause]

tone

First woman: I must admit that I was extremely reluctant. You know I don't go out much these days, I don't see many people and I tend to think that anything with more than a handful of people will be noisy and exhausting. But it was really pleasant. There was masses of room, lovely things to eat and drink, and when I discovered it was gone midnight I was amazed. The time had flown and I hadn't noticed.

[pause]

Second woman: Well, they said, Come on, you know how people do, so I went, I didn't want them to think I was being an old misery. After all, I don't often see them since we left college. But, I swear, that's the last time I let them drag me anywhere. I don't think they thought it was much fun either, though they wouldn't admit it of course, but I haven't been so bored for years. I should've stayed at home watching the rubbish on telly!

[pause]

Third woman: So anyway, they all decided they'd come too. And I said, 'But were you invited?' And they said, well, I don't know, they sort of implied they were. So I turned up with them and the girl who was giving the party, you don't know her, she's very nice, anyway she came to the door, and said 'Hello' to me and sort of looked at the others and then looked at me and I realised she thought I was taking advantage, and I went all hot and cold. Anyway we went in and I could see her looking at me from time to time, and I thought, well she won't ask me again, and I was longing to explain but I never had a chance. It was horrible. I'll never forgive them.

[pause]

Fourth woman: We all arrived and my friends went off to find drinks and things and I was just standing there feeling shy as usual and thinking, 'Why did I come?' And I saw this girl watching me, and I thought she'd noticed something wrong, so I was sort of checking myself in a mirror, trying not to look as if I was, then she came up and asked if I was Suzanne, and I said I was, and then she started on about my work. She knew all about it and said a lot of flattering things, in a very nice way. I enjoyed meeting her, she really made the evening for me. I wish I'd remembered to find out where she lived.

[pause]

Fifth woman: It was nearly a disaster. I mean, I wouldn't have missed the opportunity to meet him, but I'd had no idea it'd be swarming with children. And we were outdoors most of the time, so of course I was freezing, because I'd only got a shawl over my dress, trying to look smart. I needn't have bothered of course. Anyway, I, I did enjoy talking to him, although it wasn't for long enough really, and the food was wonderful. But, um, I think I'll swallow my pride and phone and check another time!

[pause]

tone

Now you'll hear Part Three again.

[The recording is repeated.]

[pause]

That's the end of Part Three.
Now turn to Part Four.

PART 4 *You will hear a conversation between two teenagers, Nick and Sandra. Decide whether statements 24 to 30 are true or false and mark your answers T for True or F for False. You now have forty-five seconds in which to look at Part Four.*

[pause]

tone

Nick: Hi, Sandra, where've you been?

Sandra: Oh, am I late? Sorry. I had to do some tidying up before I came out.

Nick: Yeah, I know. I hate getting home and finding I've still got to wash up from breakfast.

Sandra: It's not me that minds. It's my mother. She treats me like I was twelve or something. You've no idea how lucky you are to have your own place.

Nick: Well, you'd have to do it eventually, wouldn't you?

Sandra: I don't see why. It's my room, she doesn't have to come poking in there and telling me what to do.

Nick: Well, I guess if you don't mind the mess and it's just your room, then I suppose she should let you. Personally, I like to be able to find things in a hurry.

Sandra: I can find things when I want to. What really gets me is she makes me do all sorts of stupid chores every Saturday round the house.

Nick: Well, she can't do them all.

Sandra: She isn't going anywhere. She's got all weekend to do them.

Nick: Oh, come on. Why should she do housework all weekend while you enjoy yourself?

Sandra: She hasn't got exams next month. I haven't got time.

Nick: I think you're being a bit unreasonable. You have time to come and meet me.

Sandra: That's different.

Nick: No, it isn't.

Sandra: Whose side are you on, here?

Nick: Look, perhaps I just have a better idea how much your Mum has to get through. When you're responsible for a place it makes a lot of difference.

Sandra: Oh, don't be such a pain. Are you going to keep lecturing me all evening or are we going to see this band?

Nick: Sure. Have you brought the tickets?

Sandra: What tickets?

Nick: I got them on Thursday and gave them to you to look after. Don't you remember? You put them in your jeans pocket.

Sandra: You're teasing me. Oh no! Mum washed these jeans yesterday. I bet she never checked the pockets. Oh, I'll kill her!

Nick: Well, have a look. Anyway, I don't see why she should check your pockets.

Sandra: Okay, okay. Don't start that again. Oh no, wait a minute, this might be them. Do you think they're all right? They're a bit crumpled.

Nick: Honestly! Next time I'd better look after them myself. I'm sure they'll be OK. Now, get a move on, or we won't get in after all this.

[pause]

tone

Now you'll hear Part Four again.

[The recording is repeated.]

[pause]

That is the end of Part Four.
There'll now be a pause of five minutes for you to copy your answers onto the separate answer sheet.
I'll remind you when there's one minute left, so that you're sure to finish in time.

[pause]

You have one more minute left.

[pause]

That's the end of the test. Please stop now. Your supervisor will now collect all the question papers and answer sheets.
Goodbye.

Test 2 Key

Paper 1 Reading

Part 1
1 C   2 H   3 D   4 A   5 G   6 F   7 B

Part 2
8 C   9 C   10 B   11 A   12 C   13 D   14 B   15 A

Part 3
16 G   17 A   18 C   19 E   20 D   21 B

Part 4
22 B   23 D   24 E   25 H   26 and 27 G/H   28 A
29 D   30 C   31 B   32 E   33 and 34 A/E   35 C
(Where there are two possible answers, these are interchangeable.)

Paper 3 Use of English

Award one mark for each correct answer, except in Part 3, where two marks are available, divided up as shown, for each answer.

Correct spelling is essential throughout. Ignore omission or abuse of capital letters. No half marks.

Part 1
1 C   2 D   3 A   4 B   5 D   6 B   7 A   8 A
9 C   10 D   11 A   12 B   13 A   14 C   15 D

Part 2
16 as   17 how/what   18 it   19 into/to/through   20 or/and
21 since   22 by   23 the/those   24 of   25 been   26 In
27 are   28 this   29 which   30 fact

Part 3
31 whose coat (1) this (1) OR whose (1) this coat (1)
32 prevented her (1) (from) taking (1)
33 must not be (1) ridden (1) OR must be (1) pushed/carried/wheeled (1)
34 was amazed (1) to find (1)
35 don't need to/needn't/need not (1) book (1)
36 too high (1) for (any of) (1)
37 would/'d rather (1) you started (1)
38 they remembered (1) what (they had) (1)

46

39 hardly ever (1) loses her (1)
40 have/'ve run (1) out of (1)

Part 4

41 for   **42** the   **43** of   **44** ✓   **45** ✓   **46** more   **47** will
48 much   **49** ✓   **50** ever   **51** only   **52** ✓   **53** a   **54** at
55 it

Part 5

56 settlement   **57** southern   **58** earliest   **59** uninhabited
60 surrounded   **61** building   **62** religious   **63** successfully
64 development   **65** central

Paper 4 Listening

Part 1

1 B   **2** A   **3** C   **4** A   **5** C   **6** C   **7** A   **8** B

Part 2

9 (in the) suburbs   **10** librarian   **11** (about) once a week
12 should (stay) open later   **13** too high/not cheap   **14** need modernising
15 (more) showers   **16** athletics   **17** local business(es)   **18** pensioners

Part 3

19 C   **20** D   **21** E   **22** B   **23** A

Part 4

24 T   **25** F   **26** F   **27** T   **28** T   **29** F   **30** F

Transcript   *First Certificate Practice Test Two. Paper Four. Listening. Hello, I'm going to give you the instructions for this test. I'll introduce each part of the test and give you time to look at the questions. At the start of each piece, you'll hear this sound:*

tone

You'll hear each piece twice.
Remember, while you're listening, write your answers on the question paper. You'll have time at the end of the test to copy your answers onto the separate answer sheet.
The tape will now be stopped. Please ask any questions now, because you must not speak during the test.

[pause]

PART 1 *Now, open your question paper and look at Part One.*
You'll hear people talking in eight different situations. For questions 1 to 8,
choose the best answer, A, B or C.

Question 1 One
You are walking round a market when you hear this woman talking to a
customer. What is she doing?
A asking the customer's opinion
B offering a cheap sample
C explaining a price rise

[pause]

tone

Market trader: Look, I tell you what. You just take a couple home tonight, I'll knock off fifty pence,
how's that? And try them – you'll love 'em, I promise you – and then tomorrow you can
come and tell me if I'm not right. What d'you say to that, then? I can't say fairer than
that, now can I?

[pause]

tone

[The recording is repeated.]

[pause]

Question 2 Two
You're in the doctor's waiting room when you overhear the nurse on the
phone. Why didn't she send off the notes?
A She didn't know they were wanted.
B It isn't part of her job to do it.
C She didn't know which notes to send.

[pause]

tone

Nurse: No, I haven't received anything. ... Well, I do, normally, but even if our receptionist had,
she'd have told me straight away. ... Of course I'll go and look the notes out now and
send them off straight away. Now, what was the patient's name again?

[pause]

tone

[The recording is repeated.]

[pause]

Question 3 Three
You're in a gallery when you hear these women talking. What are they
looking at?
A a bowl
B a lamp
C a vase

[pause]

tone

First woman:	It's very lovely, isn't it?
Second woman:	Well, I suppose so, but it's not really practical, is it? I mean, it's so tall and thin you'd be afraid of knocking it over. Or would you actually put flowers in it?
First woman:	Oh, really! You'd put it somewhere where the light could shine through, just to look at it. You wouldn't want to use it. Not at that price!

[pause]

tone

[The recording is repeated.]

[pause]

Question 4   *Four*
You are visiting a large company and you hear two people talking. What are they discussing?
A a personal computer
B a typewriter
C a CD player

[pause]

tone

Woman:	Look, we can put it here on the table.
Man:	Yes, that'll leave the desk clear for papers and things. But, er, will the light be OK? You don't want it reflecting on the screen.
Woman:	No, that's all right. I can turn it at an angle. Shall I go and get the disks and things?
Man:	No, don't bother, I'll bring them up later.

[pause]

tone

[The recording is repeated.]

[pause]

Question 5   *Five*
Listen to this clerk at a station booking office. Which is the cheapest ticket?
A a period return
B an ordinary return
C a Rover

[pause]

tone

| Railway clerk: | Well, you can either get a period return, if you're going to be away more than three nights, or you can get an ordinary return that leaves you free to come back any time, but of course it costs more, although it's cheaper than two singles, of course. Or you can get a Rover ticket, which allows unlimited travel within the region for up to seven |

days. That's cheaper than the period return, and you can go further, but of course not at rush hours.

[pause]

tone

[The recording is repeated.]

[pause]

Question 6   *Six*
These friends are talking about a film. Who will go to see it?
A both of them
B neither of them
C the girl

[pause]

tone

Girl: I really think you ought to give it a chance. You aren't usually so narrow-minded.
Boy: I'm not. But Barry said his Dad really enjoyed it. We've got no tastes in common I ever heard about, so I know what it'll be like.
Girl: Well, I think you're silly. You'll be sorry when I tell you how funny it was.

[pause]

tone

[The recording is repeated.]

[pause]

Question 7   *Seven*
These people are talking about a colleague. What's his problem?
A His boss is unfair to him.
B He has been ill.
C He has too much to do.

[pause]

tone

Man: I don't know what Jim's got to grumble about. My workload has doubled in the past year and I still manage. He's not doing any different from when he arrived, as far as I can see.
Woman: Yeah, but he's not as energetic as you are. Well, no one is. But Mr Craddock doesn't tell me off when I get a bit behind, he's very understanding with me. But with Jim, he goes on and on.
Man: I haven't noticed it, but you're probably right. I wonder why he does it?

[pause]

tone

[The recording is repeated.]

[pause]

Question 8   *Eight*
Listen to this woman phoning a travel agent. What does she want to do?
A cancel her booking
B postpone her holiday
C change her destination

[pause]

tone

Woman: … on the fourth of June … Yes. Amsterdam, Holland … Now, my problem is, my brother's there, and he was supposed to be fixing accommodation for me but he has a problem with his work right now and he asked me to reserve it from here … Yeah, well what it is, I don't really want to spend my vacation going around the city alone. So I wanted to ask you whether it would cost a lot to alter the flight, say till later in the summer, when maybe he'll be freer, and we might even get to visit a few more places?

[pause]

tone

[The recording is repeated.]

[pause]

That's the end of Part One.
Now turn to Part Two.

PART 2   *You will hear an interview about sports facilities. For questions 9 to 18 fill in the answers on the questionnaire. You now have forty-five seconds in which to look at Part Two.*

[pause]

tone

Woman: Excuse me, I'm doing some research on behalf of the local Sports Committee. Would you mind answering a few questions?
Man: Well, if it won't take too long, OK.
Woman: Thanks. Um, first of all, are you a local resident?
Man: Well, more or less. It's just south of the ring road.
Woman: Oh, right, so I could put you down as 'in the suburbs'?
Man: Yes.
Woman: And are you a student, or …?
Man: I've just started work actually. I'm a librarian.
Woman: Oh, yes? And do you use the public swimming pool regularly?
Man: About once a week, I suppose, though it might be less in winter.
Woman: Right. And what do you think about the hours it opens? Should it be open later, for example?
Man: Yes, I think it should. I'd use it more often if I could go later in the evening, and I think some of my friends would too.
Woman: Uh-huh. How about the cost? Are the charges reasonable?

Man:	Well, I can afford them now I'm earning, but it's not cheap, and considering it's not particularly luxurious, I think they're a bit too high, really. Especially for school kids and families.
Woman:	Mm. So you think the facilities could be improved?
Man:	Yes, they definitely need modernising. Apart from the odd coat of paint, they haven't changed since I was a kid. When I was in Birmingham the other week I went to a pool there and I couldn't believe the difference.
Woman:	Is there anything in particular you'd like to see added?
Man:	There definitely aren't enough showers! Anyone can tell you that!
Woman:	Yes, they do! And um, do you think there are any other sports which should be catered for locally but which aren't at the moment?
Man:	Well, the sports centre is good, although it's not all that big, but like most towns you haven't really got access to anywhere for athletics unless you travel to somewhere really big. And that's no good for kids who want to train regularly.
Woman:	Yes, I agree. And there's no coaching available either, once they get beyond a certain level, is there? Anyway, we must get on. If there could be some modernisation to the pool, or other sports facilities could be improved, do you have any opinion about how that should be paid for?
Man:	Well, that's the problem, isn't it? Personally, I wouldn't mind paying a bit more tax, if it would actually get spent on the right things. But I'm young and single and I can afford to say that. Really I think the Sports Committee need to get local businesses involved. That's probably the only practical possibility.
Woman:	Right. And – I've nearly done – there've been suggestions that some groups should be able to use the pool without charge. Do you agree with this, and if so who should that be?
Man:	I visited Australia last year and I discovered that where I was staying, pensioners could get in for nothing. I think that's a really good idea. And long term it could save on doctor's bills, couldn't it?
Woman:	I suppose it might. Well thank you very much for your help.
Man:	That's OK. Bye.
Woman:	Goodbye … Excuse me, I'm doing some research on behalf of the local Sports …

[pause]

tone

Now you'll hear Part Two again.

[The recording is repeated.]

[pause]

That's the end of Part Two.
Now turn to Part Three.

PART 3   *You will hear five people talking to someone they have just met. For questions 19 to 23, choose which of the people A to F each speaker is talking to. Use the letters only once. There is one extra letter which you do not need to use. You now have 30 seconds in which to look at Part Three.*

[pause]

tone

First woman:	I've never done anything like this before, have you?
Second woman:	Er, no.
First woman:	I mean I always thought that organised tours meant bunches of foreigners buzzing around with cameras saying, 'If it's Wednesday this must be Copenhagen'. But with such a small number you don't really feel we're tourists in that sense, do you?

[pause]

Woman:	Come to join the madhouse? This is my little corner here, and I think you'll find you're just round here.
Man:	Oh, thanks.
Woman:	Now I expect you'll want a few minutes to sort your stuff out, then I'll take you round and show you where everything is. OK?
Man:	Yes. Thank you very much.

[pause]

First man:	Have you ever been on one of these before? My boss says it'll make all the difference. Well, I think she hopes it will! I'm hopeless at time management.
Second man:	Oh?
First man:	Quite posh sort of place this, isn't it? I suppose that's the chap who's going to tell us what to do. It'd better be good. It's costing our companies quite a bit to send us.
Second man:	Mm.

[pause]

First woman:	I do hope you're going to like it here. We were so glad when we heard it'd been sold. It's not nice being near an empty place for so long. We've always found people to be very friendly, and you know, we help each other out with little jobs around the place. You're not married, are you?
Second woman:	Er, well.
First woman:	Well, do drop round any time if you want a hand with anything, or you need to know where to go for anything.
Second woman:	Thanks.

[pause]

Man:	Well, that's about it really. I hope you'll find it suits you. As I said, any queries, just call me and I'll see what I can sort out.
Woman:	Thanks.
Man:	And if you do decide to use the little room as an office, just let me know and I'll get the bed out and I'll bring you a desk.
Woman:	Right, thanks.
Man:	Anyway, I expect you want to get your stuff sorted out, so if you just give me your cheque for the first month, I'll hand over your keys and leave you to it.

[pause]

tone

Now you'll hear Part Three again.

[The recording is repeated.]

[pause]

That's the end of Part Three.
Now turn to Part Four.

PART 4 *You will hear a discussion between Andy and Sharon about advertising their small business. For questions 24 to 30, decide which of the statements are true and which are false and write T for True or F for False in the box provided. You now have forty-five seconds in which to look at Part Four.*

[pause]

tone

Andy:	What was it you wanted to discuss, Sharon?
Sharon:	Well, it's this thing about advertising, Andy. I think we need to get information about ourselves across to possible customers, otherwise we're just not going to increase sales.
Andy:	OK. We both accept we're going to have to spend more in order to get business. So, let's look at the situation. We've already paid out quite a bit for that advertisement in *Local Business News*. Everyone says it was a great little advertisement, they all like it when we show it to them. Do you think it was worth it?
Sharon:	That's the problem. We don't really know. But I suspect not. Because we need to reach the guys working in the offices, staff, whatever, and that magazine lies about in reception areas for bored customers.
Andy:	Yeah, I'm sure you're right. The woman who persuaded us to take that ad out was just after what she could get. We shouldn't have listened to her. What I think we should do is advertise in the local paper.
Sharon:	Oh, come on Andy, that rag!
Andy:	Yeah, I rang them and we thought that on the same page as jobs are advertised, under Business Services. So people who're, you know, just flicking through to see if there are any better jobs going, you know, everyone does it, they see this little ad, and think, Yeah, that'd be handy for us.
Sharon:	OK. Could we afford it every day?
Andy:	I thought every Thursday. That's when the most job adverts are in. They said they'd give quite a good discount if we have a long series, say for a few months.
Sharon:	Right, that's good. Anything else? I mean, what if we got some leaflets printed and stuck them through letterboxes?
Andy:	It could be very effective, but I think there's one big disadvantage.
Sharon:	Oh?
Andy:	Well, it'd take ages to deliver them all. We've got little enough time as it is.
Sharon:	But if we paid someone else to do it?
Andy:	Who, for example? It'd be too small scale for them to want to do. Anyway, we couldn't afford a professional firm.
Sharon:	Yeah, well, I'm not so sure of that. But anyway, what about getting some students to do it? It'd be a great way for them to earn a bit of money.
Andy:	Yeah, and I know just what'd happen. They'd stick the whole lot through the first five doors and push off home. We'd never be able to keep a check on them.
Sharon:	Oh, I don't know. Well, perhaps you're right. OK, let's look at the figures for the newspaper and then see whether we could afford anything else.

[pause]

tone

Now you'll hear Part Four again.

[The recording is repeated.]

[pause]

That is the end of Part Four.
There'll now be a pause of five minutes for you to copy your answers onto the separate answer sheet.
I'll remind you when there's one minute left, so that you're sure to finish in time.

[pause]

You have one more minute left.

[pause]

That's the end of the test. Please stop now. Your supervisor will now collect all the question papers and answer sheets.
Goodbye.

Test 3 Key

Paper 1 Reading

Part 1

1 E   2 G   3 C   4 H   5 A   6 F   7 B

Part 2

8 C   9 D   10 A   11 C   12 B   13 A   14 C   15 B

Part 3

16 G   17 D   18 A   19 C   20 B   21 F

Part 4

22 and 23 A/B   24 D   25 and 26 A/D   27 B   28 C
29 and 30 A/C   31 A   32 A   33 C   34 B   35 A
(Where there are two possible answers, these are interchangeable.)

Paper 3 Use of English

Award one mark for each correct answer, except in Part 3, where two marks are available, divided up as shown, for each answer.

   Correct spelling is essential throughout. Ignore omission or abuse of capital letters. No half marks.

Part 1

1 C   2 B   3 B   4 C   5 A   6 B   7 D   8 B   9 A
10 C   11 A   12 D   13 B   14 A   15 C

Part 2

16 to   17 an/the   18 make   19 with/under/in   20 what
21 at   22 as   23 while/when/if   24 both   25 but/whereas
26 is   27 this   28 than   29 not   30 can

Part 3

31 isn't/'s/is not worth (1) asking (1)
32 would not/wouldn't/did not/didn't let/refused to let (1) him buy/get (1)
33 where she had left (1) her (1)
34 way (1) John behaved (1)
35 if you (1) had not/hadn't lent (1)
36 no notice (1) of his doctor's (1)
37 in addition (1) to writing (1)
38 during/of (1) his childhood (1)

39 don't we/not (1) go to/go and visit (1)
40 had difficulty (in) (1) concentrating on (1)

Part 4

41 a   **42** ✓   **43** near   **44** one   **45** they   **46** ✓   **47** the
48 away   **49** about   **50** since   **51** in   **52** an   **53** ✓
54 no   **55** much

Part 5

56 width   **57** height   **58** disagreement   **59** pressure
60 popularity   **61** Unfortunately   **62** wonderful   **63** requirements
64 inhabitants   **65** rarely

Paper 4 Listening

Part 1

1 A   **2** A   **3** A   **4** B   **5** A   **6** C   **7** C   **8** B

Part 2

9 Thursday(s)   **10** gallery   **11** photography   **12** print technology
13 model making   **14** academic secretary   **15** third year
16 stationery/notebooks   **17** administration assistant   **18** Department Head

Part 3

19 D   **20** A   **21** E   **22** C   **23** B

Part 4

24 C   **25** A   **26** B   **27** B   **28** A   **29** C   **30** B

Transcript *First Certificate Practice Test Three. Paper Four. Listening. Hello, I'm going to give you the instructions for this test. I'll introduce each part of the test and give you time to look at the questions. At the start of each piece, you'll hear this sound:*

tone

You'll hear each piece twice.
Remember, while you're listening, write your answers on the question paper. You'll have time at the end of the test to copy your answers onto the separate answer sheet.
The tape will now be stopped. Please ask any questions now, because you must not speak during the test.

[pause]

PART 1   *Now, open your question paper and look at Part One. You'll hear people talking in eight different situations. For questions 1 to 8, choose the best answer, A, B or C.*

Question 1   *One*
You are visiting a trade exhibition when you hear a speaker at one of the stands. What is he demonstrating?
A a watch
B a lock
C a burglar alarm

[pause]

tone

Salesman: … and now I do up the strap, see, it clicks in and it's securely held. That won't slip, whatever you do, and as I said, you can't really damage it. Water's no problem, and if you leave if off and someone else tries to walk off with it, he'll soon regret it because of the high-pitched whistle which only you can de-activate …

[pause]

tone

[The recording is repeated.]

[pause]

Question 2   *Two*
This girl is talking about a party. What was it like?
A boring
B too crowded
C noisy

[pause]

tone

Girl: No, I wouldn't bother. The last one was useless. She'd made all this food, like she was expecting about fifty people, and then hardly anyone turned up, and her music system is useless, so unless you were next to it, you practically couldn't hear the music well enough to dance even though it was turned right up. It was dead dull, basically.

[pause]

tone

[The recording is repeated.]

[pause]

Question 3   *Three*
Listen to this hotel receptionist talking on the phone. Who is she talking to?
A a friend
B a guest
C her employer

[pause]

tone

Hotel
receptionist: … row about eleven o'clock. So old George went on up, thinking it was a burglar, and
he was going to march him off … Anyway it was this Mr Hardiman, he'd locked himself
out and he was trying to force the door! You should've seen George's face … That's
right. And all the heads popping round their doors. Were we grateful the boss was away
for the night!

[pause]

tone

[The recording is repeated.]

[pause]

Question 4   *Four*
You hear this advertisement on the radio. Who is it aimed at?
A people who have plenty of money
B people who might borrow money
C people who need to save money

[pause]

tone

Woman: Close your eyes and picture yourself in a beautiful dining-room. The table is dark wood,
polished to a deep shine. The silver and glassware are reflected in the beautiful mirror
hanging above the sideboard. Long curtains in rich brocade frame the window. Now,
open your eyes and look around you. Fancy a change? It could all be yours with a loan
from Home Finance Services. Just ring 0800 2323, that's 0800 2323 for details of our
very competitive rates.

[pause]

tone

[The recording is repeated.]

[pause]

Question 5   *Five*
*Listen to these students talking about their holiday work. Where are they
working?*
A a library
B an office
C a shop

[pause]

tone

Student 1: … so then he just came up to me and said, 'Isn't it time you knew how to classify
reference books?' He can be really mean.

Student 2:   I know, and he makes you do the evenings when there's no one else there so you can't really stop people taking things out which aren't for external loans, and then he blames you because things are missing.

Student 1:   So, I said, 'But at least I understand how the computer works!'

Student 2:   I bet that got him.

Student 1:   Yeah. He went all red and didn't speak to me for hours.

[pause]

tone

[The recording is repeated.]

[pause]

Question 6   *Six*
Listen to this man. Where has he been?
A to the gym
B to the dentist
C to the barber

[pause]

tone

Man: Just don't ask! It was the usual story. You go in and say, 'Look, I just want a trim, tidy up a few straggly ends'. You know. Next thing you know you're imprisoned in this chair while some madman is let loose on you and you end up looking like this! No, it's not funny.

[pause]

tone

[The recording is repeated.]

[pause]

Question 7   *Seven*
You hear this woman talking on the radio. What is she discussing?
A music
B a picture
C architecture

[pause]

tone

Woman: ... I've got nothing against simple forms. Some of the most dramatic views in the world are created by a harmonious arrangement of very simple forms. That's fine. But this, this isn't simplicity, it's, it's flatness. It's painted in the dullest shades which are quite inappropriate to this climate. It's out of tune with its surroundings, and worst of all, I suspect, it will be unpleasant to work in as well as being an eyesore for people who have to pass by it every day.

[pause]

tone

[The recording is repeated.]

[pause]

Question 8   *Eight*
You hear this man talking to a shop assistant. Why is he annoyed?
A His pen has leaked in his pocket.
B His pen has been repaired recently.
C His pen was very expensive.

[pause]

tone

Man: Look, I realise it's not exactly the top of the range – it wasn't particularly expensive or anything, but you had it in for a repair only a fortnight ago and that cost far more than it should have done and then yesterday it started leaking when I was using it and made the most incredible mess. If it had done that in my pocket, it could have ruined an expensive suit. It really isn't on, you know!

[pause]

tone

[The recording is repeated.]

[pause]

That's the end of Part One.
Now turn to Part Two.

PART 2   *You will hear a teacher telling new students about their course. For questions 9 to 18 listen to what she says and complete the notes. You now have thirty seconds in which to look at Part Two.*

[pause]

tone

Teacher: Well, I'm very glad to welcome you all to the practical module of our Design course at the beginning of a new year. As you've no doubt realised, we have people here from years one to three, and we find that as most of the work is in small groups or individually-based, this works out pretty well, even though we're a bit short of space. Now I'm going to go through some administrative stuff and then we'll get on to project planning. So, first of all, hm, we're in the Studio here every afternoon except one, so we do have a sort of base, which is quite nice, but once a week we have to move out, that's into Room 51, which is on Thursdays. It's a bit of a nuisance, because it's not as big as in here, but we manage somehow. And on Fridays you can use the big space over the back of the hall, which is called the Gallery, for private study if you want to spread out a bit. That's only on Fridays though, I'm afraid. Now as far as extra courses go. You should've already selected these, and the days for them are as follows: um, Mondays is the only day when the darkroom is free, so that's photography. Tuesdays John Howard comes in here to take the sessions on Print Technology, and

Wednesdays I'm here for Model-making. Now if you haven't selected your options for this term, you need to get a move on. When we finish now, I'll be showing you round the rest of the department and you can get a form from the academic secretary on the way. Oh, you also need to get one if you want to do the full-day course, which is on Saturdays on Computer-aided Design. But that only applies to you third-year students, of course, and you know where the office is.

Now, that's nearly all, except a reminder to you all that we provide all the equipment you need for practical work, including card and photographic papers, but you must bring your own stationery. You should have proper notebooks, and we don't expect to have to find bits of paper for you to make notes on when you forget them. And, lastly, about absence. If you're not well, if it's just a couple of days, you can phone the administration assistant, ask him to pass a message on to this department. If it's more than a couple of days, you must send a written explanation to the Department Head otherwise you could be penalised in your course grade for absence without permission. OK? Well you have been warned. Now, for you new guys, let's go and look round the rest of the place. The rest of you no doubt have things to be getting on with.

[pause]

tone

Now you'll hear Part Two again.

[The recording is repeated.]

[pause]

That's the end of Part Two.
Now turn to Part Three.

PART 3   *You will hear five people saying thank you. For questions 19 to 23, choose which of A to F each speaker is talking about. Use the letters only once. There is one extra letter which you do not need to use. You now have 30 seconds in which to look at Part Three.*

[pause]

tone

Man: This is not an occasion where it is easy for me to know what to say. I realised of course that I wouldn't get away without some kind of little memento. After all, we've been together a long time and I know what a generous bunch you are. But I had absolutely no idea that it was going to be something like this. It's quite magnificent. Really, I'm lost for words. Except that I'm beginning to think I'll have to move house. It's so grand it'll make the rest of the place look terrible in comparison! Thank you all very, very much.

[pause]

Woman: I just called to say thank you. I've just had my results. And I know I'd never have done so well if you hadn't been pushing me this last term! ... Well, it's nice of you to say so, but honestly, I never even found the subject interesting until I got into your class.

[pause]

Man: Anyway, thanks very much for putting me on to them. They were just the right people for the job. I don't know why nobody here had heard of them. But as the boss says, 'If you want to know anything about anything, all you have to do is ask Carole! She's got all the answers.' Many thanks, and let me know if ever I can help you out some way.

[pause]

Man: Well, I certainly owe you one this time. Thank you very much indeed for telling me what might happen. It would have been a total disaster if I'd let them take it away. I think you've just saved me a lot of money. And listen, if I can do anything for you, all you have to do is name it!

[pause]

Woman: I'd like to take this opportunity to thank all of you for your hard work over the past few months. I don't need to tell you but, er, I want you to be sure that I know too, that without you guys here doing all the routine, and not so routine, work, and doing it without much understanding from outside, so that I could get on with my stuff – well, I wouldn't have achieved anything. It was a tough job for all of us and I won't forget what you've all done for me, I promise.

[pause]

tone

Now you'll hear Part Three again.

[The recording is repeated.]

[pause]

That's the end of Part Three.
Now turn to Part Four.

PART 4 *You will hear a radio discussion about a wildlife park. For questions 24 to 30, decide which of the choices, A, B or C is the correct answer. You now have one minute in which to look at Part Four.*

[pause]

tone

Gary: Now, I have with me here this evening two people who are both very interested in the future of Glenside Park. Helen, you represent the management committee of the park, and Ian (Good evening.), you represent the residents of the village of South Glen which lies just beyond the park and through which the main road into the park passes. I understand that the residents aren't too happy about some of your plans, Helen. Could you just give us an outline of what exactly these are?

Helen: Well, yes, I'm very happy to explain because I think part of the problem that has arisen is that some people in South Glen have got the wrong idea about our plans. Once they see what we're trying to do here, I think they'll agree it's a very sensible way forward.

Ian: We see perfectly well, we just don't happen to think you're right ...

Gary: OK, Ian, Ian, you'll have your say in a minute. Now, Helen, what exactly is it you're proposing?

Helen: Yes. As you know, Glenside has two problems at the moment. First, we're short of money, and second we've got too many people wandering about in parts of the park where animals, especially the birds, are trying to raise their young, disturbing them and sometimes causing the young to be left by their parents, so the staff have to try and save them by raising them by hand, which takes up precious time and, of course, is expensive.

Gary: So what do you want to do?

Helen: We think the best way to raise money would be to have more visitors to the park who'd be prepared to pay to see the animals.

Ian: But that's ridiculous! (No, it's not.) On the one hand you're accusing people of upsetting the animals, and then the next minute you're saying you want more people wandering about.

Helen: No, the point is that at the moment, people walk all over the place, they don't keep to the roads, they scare the birds, and there's a constant danger that a fire might be started and we wouldn't be able to do anything because we wouldn't know until it was too late.

Ian: Wait a minute, wait a minute. What are you talking about? People from the village would no more want to damage the park than you do!

Helen: I don't mean they'd do it on purpose. But there are such things as accidents.

Ian: Oh, come on – how many fires have you had in the last ten years?

Helen: I'm not saying we have, just that we might. Now, what we want is to have fixed routes through the park, so that visitors can be taken through and have things pointed out and explained ...

Ian: And where might these people park, may one enquire? Because it won't help relations with the village if all the roads through it are blocked with tourist cars and buses and we can't even walk through the woods where our parents and grandparents have been able to walk for generations, without paying for the honour!

Gary: He has got a point there, I think, Helen. After all, it would be quite a revolutionary plan, wouldn't it?

Helen: But people can't expect something for nothing. No, they could get tickets for a season, so they wouldn't have to queue. But they'd have to learn to respect the wildlife.

Ian: Look, tell me one example of serious harm which has been done by a local resident. We've been here for years before you turned up. If we didn't respect the land and the living things on it, it wouldn't be here for people like you to move in and start making profits out of. What have you ever done for South Glen?

Gary: OK, OK, OK, well, well, I can see that we're going to have a lot more discussion about this before the plans are carried out. (Yeah.) There is going to be a public meeting next Wednesday at South Glen Community Centre and I'm sure it'll be well-attended. Now, I think perhaps we need some music to calm us down, so here's a little tune I'm sure ...

[pause]

tone

Now you'll hear Part Four again.

[The recording is repeated.]

[pause]

That is the end of Part Four.
There'll now be a pause of five minutes for you to copy your answers onto the separate answer sheet.

I'll remind you when there's one minute left, so that you're sure to finish in time.

[pause]

You have one more minute left.

[pause]

That's the end of the test. Please stop now. Your supervisor will now collect all the question papers and answer sheets.
Goodbye.

Test 4 Key

Paper 1 Reading

Part 1
1 D   2 F   3 A   4 H   5 B   6 G   7 E

Part 2
8 D   9 D   10 A   11 A   12 B   13 C   14 B

Part 3
15 E   16 F   17 B   18 G   19 C   20 H   21 A

Part 4
22 and 23 A/C   24 D   25 C   26 B   27 A   28 and 29 B/D
30 A   31 D   32 A   33 and 34 B/D   35 E
(Where there are two possible answers, these are interchangeable.)

Paper 3 Use of English

Award one mark for each correct answer, except in Part 3, where two marks are available, divided up as shown, for each answer.

Correct spelling is essential throughout. Ignore omission or abuse of capital letters. No half marks.

Part 1
1 C   2 D   3 B   4 B   5 D   6 A   7 C   8 B   9 A
10 D   11 C   12 B   13 D   14 C   15 B

Part 2
16 another *(allow* each/every); [*not* a]   17 of   18 a   19 it   20 for   21 who   22 became [*not* was]   23 would   24 By   25 have   26 may/might   27 which/that   28 capable   29 Until/Till   30 in

Part 3
31 (that) Brenda (1) waited/(should) wait (1)
   or to Brenda (1) she should wait/(that) she wait(ed); [Brenda to wait = 0]
32 not (1) waking/getting up (1)
33 first time (1) I have/I've eaten (1)
34 managed (1) to arrest (1)
35 ought to have (1) written (1)
36 has (1) such small handwriting (that) (1)

37 have to/must (1) be picked up (1)
38 regret telling him (1) our plans (1)
39 everyone's surprise (,) (1) Geoff left (1)
40 I was to blame (1) for (1)

Part 4

41 ✓   42 still   43 so   44 a   45 ✓   46 as   47 the
48 when   49 for   50 it   51 also   52 ✓   53 well
54 ourselves   55 ✓

Part 5

56 speaking   57 preparation   58 encouraged   59 ensure
60 correctly   61 liking   62 tastiest   63 dangerous
64 importance   65 heavily

Paper 4 Listening

Part 1

1 A   2 C   3 A   4 C   5 B   6 A   7 A   8 B

Part 2

9 (beautiful, sandy) beach   10 medium-sized   11 drive/car
12 June   13 (enormous) cliffs   14 tiny   15 coach   16 model village
17 drive/car   18 winter

Part 3

19 D   20 A   21 E   22 B   23 C

Part 4

24 A   25 C   26 C   27 A   28 C   29 S   30 S

Transcript *First Certificate Practice Test Four. Paper Four. Listening. Hello, I'm going to give you the instructions for this test. I'll introduce each part of the test and give you time to look at the questions. At the start of each piece, you'll hear this sound.*

tone

You'll hear each piece twice.
Remember, while you're listening, write your answers on the question paper. You'll have time at the end of the test to copy your answers onto the separate answer sheet.
The tape will now be stopped. Please ask any questions now, because you must not speak during the test.

[pause]

PART 1   *Now open your question paper and look at Part One.*
You'll hear people talking in eight different situations. For questions 1 to 8,
choose the best answer, A, B or C.

Question 1   *One*
These women are talking about a colleague. What do they feel about his
behaviour?
A It was typical of him.
B It had improved.
C It reminded them of someone else.

[pause]

tone

First woman:	Well, it was hardly surprising really, was it? D'you remember how he went on when we tried to change the booking system?
Second woman:	You'd have thought he'd invented it himself the way he was carrying on.
First woman:	This time he went right to the Section Manager. He's a real pain about that sort of thing.
Second woman:	He doesn't seem to be able to see that we're only trying to make things work better.
First woman:	Exactly. I just can't get through to him at all.

[pause]

tone

[The recording is repeated.]

[pause]

Question 2   *Two*
This man is talking about a sports event. What happened to his team?
A They won.
B They did better than he'd hoped.
C They were very unlucky.

[pause]

tone

Man: It was incredible! We'd come right up through the league from the qualifying round. I'd always known we'd had it in us if we could just get it together. And we'd been really lucky when Mike moved into the area and joined us. It made a lot of difference. And then, there we were all set for the final, everyone in top form and three men had to pull out for silly little reasons. I couldn't believe my ears when they phoned, one after another. From then on, I knew what to expect. Even the winners said luck had been on their side.

[pause]

tone

[The recording is repeated.]

[pause]

Question 3   *Three*
Listen to this man telephoning someone about his washing machine. Who is
he talking to?
A an engineer
B a friend
C the shop he bought it from

[pause]

tone

Man: … been in touch with them already and they said it's not up to them, because the guarantee doesn't cover it. So I was wondering whether it might be the sort of thing you could handle? … I don't suppose you could give me any idea of what the charge might be? … Yes, I see. The thing is, I've got some friends coming round this weekend and um … Oh, that'd be great!

[pause]

tone

[The recording is repeated.]

[pause]

Question 4   *Four*
You switch on the radio and hear this report. Where is it coming from?
A a market
B a concert hall
C a racetrack

[pause]

tone

Sports reporter: And there's a tremendous crowd here today – everyone's milling about, looking very excited. There's laughter and music and lots of chatter. I've been talking to some of the people around me and there's no doubt that there's a fair amount of money changing hands as well. And now we'll go over to Arnold Burns who's been watching the runners coming up to the start.

[pause]

tone

[The recording is repeated.]

[pause]

Question 5   *Five*
You hear this man talking about his bad back. How did he injure it?
A in a road accident
B by lifting something
C in a fight

[pause]

tone

Man: It's not much better. Thanks for asking. I wouldn't mind so much if I hadn't been trying to help someone else. You know, John was there, struggling with this damn great case and I thought, oh, I can't leave him to cope on his own, so I went over and said, 'Let's get it up onto the wheels', and I was sort of lifting, and he was pushing, and suddenly I just felt something go in my back and that was it.

[pause]

tone

[The recording is repeated.]

[pause]

Question 6

Six
You overhear these people talking about a book. What sort of book is it?
A a guidebook
B a history book
C a novel

[pause]

tone

Man: … so I asked him what he thought, 'cause he'd been there.
Woman: And so?
Man: Well, he said most of the descriptions were quite accurate. You know, the old bits of the town, they really do look like that even now. But the factual details about good value for money, he said, they're not really aimed at people like us.
Woman: How do you mean?
Man: Well, it's written for older people really, so what he says is reasonably cheap, is really quite expensive, and when he says some old inn or something is 'adequate', we'd find it really comfortable.
Woman: Perhaps I'd better see if I can find something more suitable.

[pause]

tone

[The recording is repeated.]

[pause]

Question 7

Seven
Listen to this woman who has just arrived at a meeting. Why is she late?
A The weather was bad.
B There was a traffic jam.
C She crashed her car.

[pause]

tone

Woman: I'm so sorry. I do hope you haven't been waiting to begin. It was just after I left Oxford, there was this tremendously heavy rain and all the traffic had to slow right down, you couldn't see a thing. I was convinced I was going to hit something. Anyway, I'm really sorry.

[pause]

tone

[The recording is repeated.]

[pause]

Question 8 *Eight*
At the sports club you hear these people discussing an exercise. What is its purpose?
A to help you lose weight
B to make you relax
C to strengthen the stomach muscles

[pause]

tone

Man: So, was the class any use?

Woman: It was pretty tiring! We did do some quite good things though. There was one where you had to lie on your stomach, and very gently move your arms from above your head down to your sides.

Man: Hardly very energetic!

Woman: But you feel very sort of calm afterwards. All the tension goes out of your shoulders. At least that's the idea, apparently.

[pause]

tone

[The recording is repeated.]

[pause]

That's the end of Part One.
Now turn to Part Two.

PART 2 *You will hear part of a radio programme about holidays. For questions 9 to 18, complete the grid. You now have thirty seconds in which to look at Part Two.*

[pause]

tone

Presenter: Hello and welcome to the Holiday Spot. Today we have reports on three contrasting places, all within a couple of hours of the capital. And first we have Gabrielle, who's been to Eastingham.

Gabrielle: Yes, well, I must admit I thought I was the unlucky one, getting Eastingham, but in fact I was really pleasantly surprised. I thought the main attraction would be night clubs and fast food bars. In fact it's just a medium-sized town with an old-fashioned sea front, and most of the visitors are there for the absolutely beautiful sandy beach, which is actually more impressive in reality than on the postcards. I went by road, as it didn't occur to me that I could go by train, and I must say that although it might have saved me half an hour, it would have meant quite a long walk at the other end, as the station is on the inland side of the town. Also, for a day trip, a car's a must, as the last train is a very slow one. And I had no trouble parking even though I was there in August. I was told that June is ideal, when the weather is most likely to be sunshine but the crowds haven't got too bad. Actually I suspect that Eastingham's idea of really crowded would be some resorts' idea of pleasantly lively. Um, for a relaxed day in the traditional style, Eastingham's just the place.

Presenter: Thanks, Gabrielle. Now we turn to Josh, who's been sampling the delights of Brant, just ten miles along the coast.

Josh: Yes, I've just returned from an amazing weekend. Brant is a tiny place with several excellent homely guest houses and visitors come here because it's a great base for a walking holiday. Its most exciting feature is the enormous cliffs which rear up above the sea. It's not too difficult to reach from the city, only about an hour and half's drive by coach and these go most days. It's not really a good idea to take your own car, even though the roads aren't bad, because the parking space is very restricted and during the day it's expensive. But a great place to get the traffic fumes out of your lungs.

Presenter: Thank you Josh. You certainly sound refreshed. And lastly, we hear from Catherine, who's been on a day trip to Faresey. I believe you took some friends with you, Catherine?

Catherine: Well, I'd heard that Faresey boasted an attraction which was popular with children from eight to eighty, so I took my neighbour Tom, who's twelve, and his granddad, Alec, who's seventy. And, well, the day was a roaring success. Faresey is the home of a model railway, but what really pulls in the crowds is that you can spend hours going round an entire model village, complete with market, workshops and houses, all based on Faresey in the nineteenth century. I was fascinated by it, and so were my friends. I had been worried that there wouldn't be enough to keep Tom occupied, but the working model machines really hooked him. Faresey itself is a pleasant small town, and the model village is something which you can't help being interested by. It's easy to get to if you drive, as it's just ten minutes from the motorway, about forty minutes altogether from here. And it's open all the year round. In fact, I'd recommend it as a good day out during winter rather than summer, as you could still be there and back in daylight and the crowds might be thinner, so you wouldn't have to wait for a clear view of the models. Not that that's a great problem, even in summer, but you do have to be a bit patient at some of the best bits.

Presenter: Well, it sounds as though you've all had a good time. Many thanks. And now to our foreign holiday slot. Here's Jenny …

[pause]

tone

Now you'll hear Part Two again.

[The recording is repeated.]

[pause]

That's the end of Part Two.
Now turn to Part Three.

PART 3 *You will hear five people talking about clothes. For questions 19 to 23, choose from the list A to F what each speaker is talking about. Use the letters only once. There is one extra letter which you do not need to use. You now have 30 seconds in which to look at Part Three.*

[pause]

tone

Woman: And now here is Patrick. This is beautifully cut in fine wool with hand-sewn detail on the sleeves and a flattering pleat at the waistline of the trousers. The jacket lining is of silk, making it wonderfully comfortable. This is an absolute must for winter which you'll still be wearing next spring. It's available in a range of colours, both classic and more adventurous.

[pause]

Woman: I've had it for years. Actually I think it was my grandfather's. I expect he used to wear it on expeditions. It keeps the sun out of your eyes without making your head hot. Everyone laughs at illustrations of nineteenth-century costume, but all the same they did get some things right. And this is one of them. Well, as far as I'm concerned anyway.

[pause]

Man: Well, it was pouring with rain, as you know, and when we got there I had to take my shoes off because they were absolutely soaked. It was so embarrassing. There was this great hole with my toe sticking out. I'm sure it wasn't there when I was getting dressed. It must have caught on the shoe lining and then just spread. Well, what could I do? I just laughed!

[pause]

Woman: Where does he find them? Last week he had on, I'm not joking, an open-necked, orange and pink nylon striped one. He looked like a garden chair. Jeremy said it gave him a headache looking at it all day. I don't know what the customers make of it. You'd think he'd get cold in those short sleeves too.

[pause]

Man: Yeah, I'm very pleased with it really. It's big enough to go over anything, it's really warm and it looks smart enough. I never used to bother when I drove to work, but now I'm using the train I needed something to keep out the wind and rain. That's why I have it so long. It keeps my knees dry too.

[pause]

tone

Now you'll hear Part Three again.

[The recording is repeated.]

[pause]

That's the end of Part Three.
Now turn to Part Four.

PART 4 *You will hear two friends discussing evening study courses. For questions 24 to 30, decide which course each statement refers to. Mark A for Art, or C for Computers or S for Spanish. You now have forty-five seconds in which to look at Part Four.*

[pause]

tone

Tracy: Hey, Polly, how's it going?

Polly: Hi, Tracy. Hey, I went into the Institute on my way home today to find out about evening classes. They've got some very good courses planned this year.

Tracy: Oh, did you get a leaflet?

Polly: No, they're re-printing them. But some are the same as last year, and I made a couple of notes.

Tracy: I'm not sure I really want to bother this year. It's such a drag turning out again after you get in in the evening. And that painting course had so many people in it that you couldn't really get any individual help.

Polly: Yes, well they've decided to limit the numbers this year, so if you want to do it you have to book a place. I can understand why, I suppose. Anyway I don't know, but I wonder whether I ought to do the computing really. It might be useful. I mean if I was going for promotion.

Tracy: But would it be advanced enough for you, Polly? You already do quite a lot of that sort of thing, don't you?

Polly: Oh, I think so. The woman who runs it is supposed to be very good. She's not just a programmer, she's a trained teacher as well.

Tracy: Well, it's up to you of course. Sounds like my idea of hell, at the end of a day's work. I just want something relaxing.

Polly: But Tracy, I think you really ought to do something, even if it's just the same one as last year.

Tracy: But then I'd have to pay for materials. That's another reason I don't think I want to do it again. I can't afford more than the minimum.

Polly: Well, why don't you try Spanish? It'd be easy for you, Tracy, knowing Italian, and it'd be really useful on holiday.

Tracy: Mm. Don't the language courses last two terms? I don't know I want to tie myself up for that long.

Polly: Er, I don't think so, no. That's the computer course. But they're pretty intensive so you really get through a lot in a short time.

Tracy: If it's so good, why don't you try it yourself?

Polly: I'd like to, it's just I ought to consider my career and I don't have time for both.

Tracy: Oh, well. Let's think about it over the weekend.

Polly: All right.

[pause]

tone

Now you'll hear Part Four again.

[The recording is repeated.]

[pause]

74

That is the end of Part Four.
There'll now be a pause of five minutes for you to copy your answers onto the separate answer sheet.
I'll remind you when there's one minute left, so that you're sure to finish in time.

[pause]

You have one more minute left.

[pause]

That's the end of the test. Please stop now. Your supervisor will now collect all the question papers and answer sheets. Goodbye.